More Praise for
How to Tell Anyone Anything

"People avoid difficult conversations because they want to preserve the relationship, and are afraid that saying anything will just make things worse. *How to Tell Anyone Anything* gives you the tools you need to begin these dialogues and have truly candid and painless conversations. Gallagher's strength-based approach to coaching and feedback will enhance your relationships, and bring out the best in you and your team."

—Amy Diamond Barnes,
SPHR Executive Director of Human Resources,
Washington and Lee University

"This book will dramatically change your ability to influence and lead others. At first I was skeptical, because my experience is that dealing with difficult people is almost always painful. Yet once I put Gallagher's step-by-step approach into action, I was amazed. Now, I'm solidly convinced that you can indeed have painless conversations with anyone!"

—Michelle C. Berry, CEO, Courtney Consulting;
motivational speaker, and author of *The Month of Not Speaking*

"*How to Tell Anyone Anything* takes the fear out of feedback. In fact, this book takes the 'feedback' out of feedback, by turning criticism into dialogue, and allowing managers and employees to speak together like rational adults. The book is clearly written with an approach that provides humor to what is ordinarily a very stressful topic. I recommend it for everyone in the workplace."

—Susan Shwartz, Ph.D., financial writer and marketer

HOW TO TELL ANYONE

ANYTHING

Breakthrough Techniques for Handling
Difficult Conversations at Work

RICHARD S. GALLAGHER

◢AMACOM

American Management Association
New York • Atlanta • Brussels • Chicago • Mexico City • San Francisco
• Shanghai • Tokyo • Toronto • Washington, D.C.

This publication is designed to provide accurate and authoritative information in regard to the subject matter covered. It is sold with the understanding that the publisher is not engaged in rendering legal, accounting, or other professional service. If legal advice or other expert assistance is required, the services of a competent professional person should be sought.

Library of Congress Cataloging-in-Publication Data

Gallagher, Richard S.
   How to tell anyone anything : breakthrough techniques for handling difficult conversations at work / Richard S. Gallagher.
        p.   cm.
     Includes bibliographical references and index.
     ISBN-13: 978-0-8144-1015-8
     ISBN-10: 0-8144-1015-4
     1. Business communication.   2. Interpersonal communication.   3. Conflict management. 4. Conversation. I. Title.

   HF5718.G347   2009
   658.4'5—dc22

                                                              2008045740

Printing number

10   9   8   7   6   5   4   3   2   1

*To every seminar attendee
who has ever taken me aside and asked me
how to get along better with someone —
this book is dedicated to you.*

Contents

Acknowledgments

To all of the great employees on teams I have managed, all the managers who have inspired and taught me, the friends and colleagues who have shared their energy and ideas, and the thousands of people who have attended my communications skills programs over the years—this book is as much yours as it is mine, and it reflects the many things I have learned from you.

To Martha Hubbard, Susan Greener, and their team at my local business extension TC3.biz in upstate New York—you served as a valuable test kitchen for teaching the concepts in this book to a number of very engaged and appreciative audiences. Thanks also to Susan's predecessor Beth Van Dine for planting the seed years ago of looking at strength-based versus deficit-based models of communication.

To Ginny Cutler, Larry Hanville, and everyone at EMQ Children and Family Services in Campbell, CA—your groundbreaking use of a strength-based approach with the families you serve, and the experiences we had implementing a strength-based communications model for your own team members, were both a tremendous inspiration to this book.

To Executive Editor Ellen Kadin and the entire team of professionals at AMACOM Books, and to my literary agent Diana Finch—thank you for a great working relationship that now spans four years and three books. It is a true pleasure working with all of you.

Finally, to my wife Colleen—we have always had a model of a strength-based relationship, but I still refer to it as being madly in love. Thank you for being a great editor, but more important, thank you for just being you.

A New Way of
Looking at Dialogue

"I can't *deal* with him anymore!"

This pained outburst, spoken sharply into a cell phone, rose above the din of a crowded Wednesday afternoon at Chicago's O'Hare Airport, as a well-dressed man wheeled his luggage behind me. Later that same afternoon, settling into my seat at the United Airlines Red Carpet Club, I overheard more cell phone conversations from more successful-looking people with business suits and briefcases—things like:

> "She may be the boss, but she doesn't know how to get along with anyone,"
>
> "Everyone knows that he just isn't working out, but no one has the guts to tell him,"
>
> "I got so fed up with that man that I walked out of a project with him and got fired!"

These people all have one thing in common: *they don't know how to positively influence the behavior of other people.* They struggle with how to talk with their employees, their bosses, and their peers about difficult subjects—or perhaps they have tried airing their grievances and gotten nowhere—so instead, they gripe to others and feel powerless. They don't realize that the right kind of honest and authentic communication, delivered in a nonthreatening way, could actually change many of these situations for the better. And if this group of elite frequent flyers among America's best and brightest feel stuck in situations like these, where does that leave the rest of us?

Situations like these lie at the heart and soul of our ability to engage in *dialogue*, a term the dictionary defines broadly as "an exchange of ideas and opinions" and more specifically as "a discussion between representatives of parties to a conflict that is aimed at resolution." In the ideal, dialogue serves as a mechanism to make things right. But in our own experience, it too often has the opposite effect. When we ask people to improve their performance, treat others differently, or even shower more often, the result is frequently anger and resentment—and far too often, nothing changing. So does this mean we are forever doomed to choose between getting people riled up, or swallowing our pride and accepting the status quo?

In a word: No!

This book presents what, for most people, is a very new and different approach to having difficult conversations in the workplace—one that is remarkably effective in actually getting people to listen to you, negotiate with you, and ultimately make positive changes in their behavior. This approach is easy to learn and put into practice, and is grounded in broader trends that are now changing the way we apply psychology to human situations. Above all, it is designed seemingly to achieve the impossible: to make these conversations *painless* on both sides of the discussion.

So, is there a catch to this win-win situation? Yes, just one. It will require you to *change the way you view and respond to people*—and at times, say things that are precisely the opposite of what you might have said in the past. But once you experience the results of this new approach to communicating with people, I'm betting that you'll never go back to the old way again. This new, painless approach to dialogue will not only help give you power in situations where most people feel powerless, it will fundamentally change the way you relate to other people in all areas of your life—because the techniques will work just as well with personal as with business contacts.

To give you a taste of where we are heading, let's jump right in with a real-world example that is all too common in many workplaces:

Service with a Slam!

You are the manager of a telephone customer service center, and once in a while you like to walk the floor and hear what people on your team are saying to customers. Today, as you approach Marcia's cubicle, you can hear what she is saying from 20 feet away:

"This is the fourth time I've tried to explain this to you, and all you do is keep asking more stupid questions! I've already spent way to much time trying to help you with this problem. You need to go find someone who knows what they are talking about. Goodbye!" As you walk by, you can hear her slam the receiver down and sigh deeply.

Now, what would *you* say to your employee Marcia after hearing this? Let me guess. If you are like most people, I suspect it would fall into one of three categories:

1. You would have some choice words for Marcia that you probably wouldn't say in church.
2. You would gravely intone about your company's service standards, how Marcia's behavior doesn't meet these standards, and how she needs to improve.
3. You would try to avoid a confrontation by dodging the subject entirely, but make a mental note of it for her next performance review.

Next question: how do you think Marcia will react to any of these approaches? Will she express joy and thankfulness at being shown how to do her job better? Will she enthusiastically commit to meeting standards of excellent customer service in the future? In fact, is she likely to make any positive long-term changes at all, particularly the next time you're out of earshot?

I didn't think so—and that's where this book comes in. Whenever I've been in situations like these (and as someone who spent much of his career managing call center operations, trust me, I have), here is how I have handled them, using the approach that forms the basis of this book:

- I would come to Marcia with a smile on my face, observe that this customer was getting under her skin, and ask her to tell me about it.
- As she responds to me, I would *acknowledge* and *validate* everything that she says. ("You're right. Customers who don't read the manual and take up your time are really frustrating. I hate being in situations like that too.")
- Next, I would offer to help make this situation better in a way that benefits *her*. ("Would you like to learn how I handle situations like these?")
- Finally, I would role-play better ways to handle the situation with her, and have fun with it. ("Marcia, here is a way to tell someone they are stupid without ever using the word 'stupid' in the sentence: talk about what happened when *you* made the same mistakes.")

What you are seeing here are the mechanics of a totally new way of having a difficult conversation—a positive, criticism-free process that never puts the listener on the defensive, even in difficult or sensitive situations. The results of this approach? Consistently, over and over, I've watched people with so-called "bad attitudes" blossom into top-rated employees, some of whom even garnered awards and leadership roles.

But for some of you reading this, I believe that I can read your mind right now. "Oh, come on, you're just being nice to a rude employee. You aren't holding her accountable. She isn't experiencing any consequences for her behavior!" If you work with people in the real world, these all sound like legitimate concerns—so let's look critically at each of them:

"You're just being nice to a rude employee." Actually, what you are seeing here is a very formal, scripted process that has nothing to do with my attitude. It is, in fact, a thoughtfully planned and composed performance. More important, this isn't something that I or anyone else just made up off the top of our heads, but rather a process based on very specific principles of human behavior. As you read through this book, you will learn exactly what I said at each step of this process, and why I am saying it.

"You aren't holding her accountable." Actually, if you read this carefully, I am holding her very much accountable: I am coaching her. And I will keep coaching her, again and again if needed, until her performance

meets my expectations. What I think you really mean to say is that I am not *criticizing* her, and on that point you are precisely correct.

Listen carefully. I have never accepted people giving less than their very best at their jobs, and I have the management track record to prove it, including creating near-perfect customer satisfaction ratings, near-zero external turnover, and high growth. Anyone who has worked for me for more than ten minutes knows that I have extremely high expectations for how people treat our customers, our organization, and each other. And at the end of the day, I use a painless approach to communications skills for a very selfish reason: it gets *me* much more of the behavior that *I* want in situations like these.

"She isn't experiencing any consequences for her behavior." What you are really saying is that she isn't experiencing any *punishment* for her behavior. Again, you are correct. I am 100% focused on changing how she responds to customers in the future, rather than making her feel bad about how she responded to them in the past.

One of the things you will learn as you work your way through this book is that while our natural reaction is often to lash out at people who disappoint us, criticism and punishment are almost always the *least* effective way to change performance. If you want things like sullen compliance, resentment, turnover, and sabotage, negative feedback will certainly get you there. But I want something much better for you: I want you to be able to help people grow and change.

THE THEORY BEHIND PAINLESS CONVERSATIONS

Picture an important peer in your life: perhaps your spouse or partner, a good friend, or one of your co-workers. Now, I have a question for you: have you ever tried to change his or her behavior? When I ask this question to audiences at my training programs, nearly every hand goes up (including mine). But then when I ask another equally simple question—did it work?—suddenly no one's hand is raised.

The reason for this is that most of us naturally practice "deficit-based" communications, where we point out another person's faults and try to correct them. Deficit-based feedback is simple and logical—and almost never works. Why? Because human beings are inherently programmed to fight back against criticism, no matter how "right" it is.

But there is a new approach in psychology—it's called a *strength-based* approach—that will dramatically change your ability to influence people in any situation. It isn't a gimmick, nor is it a random assortment of verbal techniques that you will need to memorize and pull out on command. Instead, it is a proven approach that is based on one simple but powerful idea:

Always speak to the other person's strengths and interests—even in difficult situations.

It is the key to effective, painless communication on any subject. Sounds simple enough, right? So why isn't everyone practicing strength-based communication already? The problem is, when we go into the real world and run head-on into challenging situations, strength-based feedback is the last thing on earth we want to do. Here is why:

- When an employee is late again, the last thing you want to do is "understand" it.
- When you feel someone is dead wrong, the last thing you want to do is explore the benefits of her approach.
- When someone is rude and abrasive, the last thing we want to ask is what frustrates *him*.

But that last thing you want to do is exactly what will keep another person in dialogue, and more often than not, change their behavior. Here is why:

- When you acknowledge the feelings and frustrations of the late employee, you can much more effectively coach him—or even discipline him.
- When another person feels you understand the benefits of her approach, it becomes much easier for them to listen to your concerns.
- When you connect with another person's frustrations, it opens the door to showing him more productive ways to handle them.

Using numerous real-life examples, this book will show you how to fundamentally change your ability to influence other people's behavior, using a simple process that creates honest, authentic dialogue that benefits everyone concerned. As I mentioned before, these powerful new communication skills have their roots in psychology; if you are interested in learning more about the psychological underpinnings of these techniques, read Appendix B. Meanwhile, let's start by looking in detail at why difficult conversations are so hard for most of us.

Section I

The Basics

CHAPTER 1

Why We Stink at Difficult Conversations— And How We Can Change

"I keep talking to him about his behavior, but he never changes."

Does this line sound familiar? I would say that it is nearly universal. We all go around with the best of intentions trying to get other people to listen to us, and usually fall flat on our faces.

Of course, we understand perfectly why *other* people don't succeed in getting people to change. Like the woman who feels she is a "perfect mother" but in reality is always criticizing her children. Or the toxic boss who rules by fear and intimidation. Or the coach who claims to have "high standards" for people when he is really just screaming at them and demoralizing them. These people clearly do not communicate well. But ourselves? Never. We are all nice people with only the best of intentions. So why doesn't anyone ever seem to listen to us?

In this chapter, we'll learn the answer to this question. First, we'll take a look at the mechanics of how we approach sensitive conversations and why we say what we usually say, and more important, why it doesn't work. Then, using a case study, I'll show you how anyone can dramatically change this and connect with anyone. In the process, you are going to start learning an approach that will help you bring dialogue much closer to its historical reason for existence— namely, to improve the lives of both you and the people around you.

CONTEXT IS EVERYTHING

So what is it that makes difficult messages so hard to give, and so much harder for people to accept? And why, given that we are all reasonably smart people, do most of us have such a low rate of success with it?

3

Many of you may be thinking that people just naturally resist being told what to do, especially when the message is not a good one. That is a simple and seemingly logical explanation. Surprisingly, it is also not a correct one. The reality is that *some* people can tell *some* people almost anything, and this fact drives how we learn to communicate with people in general. Let's look at some examples of very blunt conversations that do not fall on deaf ears.

- It is a hot summer night, and the players from a top major league baseball team are making their way into the clubhouse after a close win. As the starting pitcher comes through the door, the left fielder yells out, "Hey, Jones, you stunk in that last inning!" Jones smiles and winks as he heads to his locker.
- Your wife is the light of your life, even when she is standing in front of you on a Saturday morning with a paint brush in hand, saying, "Alright, honey, no more goofing off with your pet projects. You're going to paint the garage this weekend or else!"
- Two talented musicians are listening to the tracks they laid down at this afternoon's recording session. "Doesn't work," says one of them. "Needs more 'oomph' in the bass. And those chords don't really do it for me. This isn't your best stuff, Carol." Carol nods in agreement.

OK, let's recap. Telling a competitive professional athlete that he performed terribly. Confronting one's husband and asking him to give up his Saturday to do chores. Letting a musician know that her hard work was all for naught. These are all really bad examples of feedback, right?

No, these are actually really *good* examples of relationships. These people are all so close, personally and professionally, that they feel they can be totally honest and authentic with each other. Because the relationship between each of these people is so strong, there is little or no concern about how the other person will react; in fact, they will usually appreciate the other person's honesty. You could say that these people have a high level of *relationship strength*. As a result, their normal approach to dialogue works very well for them.

Now, let's shift gears to the workplace, and try these same conversations in a different context:

- Steve and his co-workers file back into the office after finishing a big client presentation. Melinda, the sales manager, furrows her brow as they pass by and yells out, "Steve, you really stunk up there!"

- A team leader walks up to one of her employees with a thick file in her hand and a scowl on her face. As she plops it down with a loud "thump" in the middle of his desk, she declares, "Alright, Davis, no more goofing around with your pet projects. You're going to get these accounts finished this week or else!"
- Carol and her manager, who only meet every month or so, are reviewing her latest project. He looks over her work and gravely intones, "This doesn't work for me. It needs more 'oomph' in the design. This isn't your best work, Carol."

What do you notice about these exchanges? The only real difference here is that these people lack the same closeness and camaraderie as the people we mentioned earlier. As a result, these same messages are now delivered with seriousness and distance.

Now, how do you think the receivers will feel after receiving this second round of comments? You could probably describe it with a collective "Ewwww. . . ." And if you jump ahead and try to predict their responses, you are probably on pretty safe ground expecting a lot of anger, excuses, and defensiveness.

But this *is* how most people communicate in the workplace. We hold people accountable. We expect high performance. We point out problems. We tell people to shape up or else. And then we expect them to react the same way that the ballplayers did in the clubhouse. We don't just have a communications problem; we have a perceptional problem because we think that these blunt comments will work for us like they do in our closest relationships. Now, let's look at how we got to this point, and more important, how we get out.

WHY INEFFECTIVE DIALOGUES ARE IN YOUR GENES

The reason most of us talk to people the way we do—and the reason it usually fails—is deceptively simple. Most of us grow up in a cocoon surrounded by family and close friends. Our level of relationship strength is usually very high in those early years, and it is here where we learn to interact with others.

Within that relatively safe cocoon, we are more or less free to speak our minds at will, and this is in fact how we learn to survive. When we are helpless babies, we cry when we are hungry, and we get fed. When we are toddlers and something scares us, we call out and people around us react. And when we get a bit older and tell our little brother to stop picking his nose, in all likelihood he will still hang around and continue to be your little brother afterwards. We learn very powerfully at a young age to give blunt and direct feedback because it works, and it is usually safe to do so.

There is one big exception to this, of course. We also learn that it is not OK to be blunt with people who have more authority than us. Most of us would rather not reminisce about what happened when we told our dad to shut up, or pointed out what an ugly outfit our mother was wearing. There are other exceptions as well, such as the families whose communications problems keep the family therapy industry alive and well. But for the most part, the majority of us survive adolescence feeling like we can say just about anything to anyone as long as we have a close relationship with them.

Now let's fast forward to adulthood and the workplace. Most of us are now nice, civilized, mature people—until something goes wrong and we try to talk to another person about it. Given how we are all socialized, most of us do this in a way that closely resembles how we told our little brother to stop picking his nose. In other words, we have all learned to use *high-relationship-strength* communication skills in *low-relationship-strength* situations.

We could probably best express this with a simple graph. If you take everyone in the world and lay them out on a graph, like in the figure shown here, you will see that they fall into three groups:

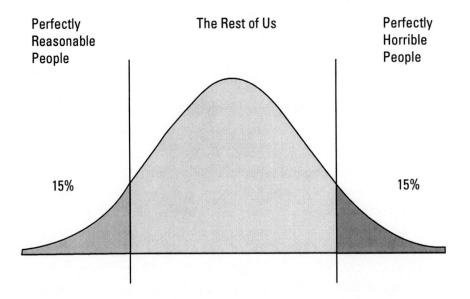

Perfectly Reasonable People   The Rest of Us   Perfectly Horrible People

15%   15%

- The first group—about 15 percent of us—are perfectly reasonable people. We have high relationship strength with these people, and almost anything we say will work with them.
- At the other end of the graph, representing another 15 percent of us, are perfectly horrible people. These are the people who cut you off in traffic, harass your employees, and cheat on their taxes. Can you influence them? Perhaps, but in general their behavior and disregard for other people's boundaries goes beyond the domain of what effective communications skills can accomplish.
- This leaves a critical mass of 70 percent of people in the middle. They are not hyper-reasonable, nor are they complete jerks. You aren't close to them like family or close friends. If you criticize them they will push back, but if you speak to their interests, you will probably have their ear.

You have just two choices if you want to influence this 70 percent majority with whom you don't already connect. One is that you can convince them to join your household for the next several years so you can get away with being very frank and straightforward with them. The other is that you learn an entirely new way of communicating with them that works much better. Now, let's take a peek at how to do this.

A Case Study: The Critic in the Corner Office

Let's take a hypothetical situation that is all too real for many people. You love your job, but you wish you could say the same for your boss, Augustus Meanie. He is blunt, intimidating, yells at people when they make mistakes, and knows exactly what buttons to push to make you feel two feet tall. Here are some of his favorite phrases:

"You call this work? A third-grader could do a better job than this!"

"So you're going to slack off on us and not work late tonight?"

"Some people are here to work, and some people are here to make work."

Now, here is your assignment: You are going to ask him to quit insulting you. Of course, he is your boss and can fire you at will. As senior vice president of Meanie International, he isn't going anywhere soon. And you have little influence over him, other than perhaps quitting.

First, let's start with what most people would say in this situation, and why it usually doesn't work:

1. *The Direct Approach*
   You: Stop insulting me!
   Mr. Meanie: I am not insulting you. I am just stating the facts. Your work is inferior.

2. *The Kiss-Up Approach*
   You: You are so right about that, Mr. Meanie. I need to do a better job on this.
   Mr. Meanie: You're darned right. Harrumph.

3. *The "Boundaries" Approach*
   You: You don't have the right to call me names like that.
   Mr. Meanie: I can call you anything I feel like calling you. Especially when you turn in lousy work like this. Now get back to work!

Each of these responses seem logical and rational on the surface, but Mr. Meanie's response is predictable for each of them. The reason is that each of them speak to *our* interests. In the first case, we are asking him to stop his unpleasant behavior. In the second case, we are transparently trying to deflect his criticism by agreeing with him, in a way that sounds artificial and forced. In the third case, we are trying to set personal boundaries for his behavior. And Mr. Meanie couldn't care less about any of these things. You are using high-relationship-strength feedback in a situation where your relationship strength is not particularly high.

Now, if you were a good friend of Mr. Meanie and asked him frankly if he was a bully, he would probably have a look of stunned surprise on his face. "Why, no, not at all," he would say. "I am just trying to get the best out of everyone who works here. If you don't hold people accountable, they'll get away with murder. That's why I don't let people get too comfortable around here—so that they don't think they're in a country club." He probably goes to bed every night and sleeps soundly, secure in the knowledge that he is doing what he feels is the best for his company.

This observation represents the key to communicating effectively—and painlessly—with Mr. Meanie. He has an agenda, and he believes in it to the soles of his wing tips. If you can speak to this agenda, you have a chance of influencing his behavior. If you don't speak to it, you have very little chance of influencing it. And if you do what 95 percent of people do in this situation, and speak to your own interests, you are probably toast.

So now, let's try an entirely different approach. For starters, here are some of the things I'd like you to say to Mr. Meanie when you begin your discussion:

"What kinds of things frustrate you about my work?"
"What does a good employee look like to you?"
"Are there specific things you see wrong in my work that we can troubleshoot?"
"What would you like to see our team accomplish in the future?"

Feel the temperature drop? Good. And please bear with me if you think we are just kissing up to Mr. Meanie again. We aren't. Instead, we are starting an important discussion in a safe place, so that it will get you where you want. Then we are asking questions designed to help you understand what goes on in Mr. Meanie's own mind.

Next, we are going to do something that feels like sucking on a lemon for most people: We are going to *acknowledge* and *validate* each and every thing Mr. Meanie says in response to you. Not just the parts we agree with, but every single utterance out of his mouth. And we will do it all afternoon if we need to. Here goes:

Mr. Meanie: You do a much sloppier job than the other technicians.

You: It must be annoying when people like me don't give you what you want.

Mr. Meanie: Look at this project, for example. My toddler could do better than this.

You: You clearly want me to meet a higher standard than I have been delivering lately.

Mr. Meanie: The problem is that people don't work hard enough around here.

You: I would be frustrated if I ran a company and felt that people didn't match my energy level on the job.

Listen carefully. You are not agreeing with this person. Nor are you prostrating yourself in subservience to him. You are doing one thing, and one thing alone: You are telling this person that you understand how he thinks, and that it is safe for him to talk about it. Even if he is a Meanie.

Some of you may have a strong emotional reaction to responses like these. It may feel totally wrong to be giving your boss any credit at all, particularly if you disagree with him and dislike his personality. That's OK. Be aware, however, that you are only acknowledging how he feels here, not signing off on it. If you read these words carefully, you have not—yet—agreed to change anything. And if you violently disagree with him about the quality of your work, you can tone down these statements even further and stick to the feelings alone: for example, "I can tell by your tone of voice you are frustrated about this." Just remember for now that you *must* find some way to acknowledge Mr. Meanie *every time* he opens his mouth, or you have very little chance of succeeding in this discussion.

Now we get to the fun part. Remember the original purpose of this discussion? It was to tell him to stop yelling at you. Now we get to hit that issue right between the eyes. Here we go:

"I want to do the very best job I am capable of here. I frankly want to make you and our entire team look good. I find that it is very hard for me to learn and improve when I constantly feel disrespected and criticized. What could we do to work together from here and help me give you what you want?"

Let's recap what you just said here. You minced no words about what you want. You gave him an incentive to give you what you want. And perhaps most important, you made him part of the problem-solving process rather than just making demands. You have taken a very difficult conversation, with a very difficult person, and created a painless dialogue that gives your agenda a much higher probability of success.

What you just saw doesn't involve smoke, mirrors, or cute phrases. It is a reproducible step-by-step process. It is grounded in principles of behavioral psychology that work very consistently. Above all, it gives you your very best opportunity to create real, positive changes between you and the people you work and live with changes that will lead to better working relationships, higher performance, lower stress, and fewer sleepless nights. Now, let's look at how this view of the world can change everything about how you communicate with people.

From "Difficult People" to New Relationships

Of course, not every difficult conversation involves setting boundaries with a crabby boss. Perhaps you might want to tell the nicest person in the world that she needs to do something about her breath. Or two people that you both like very much are fighting with each other like cats and dogs, and any attempt to discuss it leads to a finger-pointing marathon between them. Or someone who has a great attitude and work ethic unknowingly ticks off everyone else on his team by dominating the conversation in every meeting.

Think about all of the situations with people where you feel powerless and uncomfortable, and they probably break down into a few predictable categories:

- Someone treats you or others in a way that creates friction.
- A person has personal habits that are embarrassing to discuss.
- Someone is doing a poor job, and may or may not realize it.
- People are in conflict with each other.
- Others are blind to things that hold them back from what they want.

What does your list look like? Can you boil them down into common situations like these? And what kinds of things frustrate you when you try to deal with them?

The good news is that these are all known situations that you can understand and manage, in much the same way that we dealt with the rude manager earlier in this chapter. You don't have to change your personality, care more, or move your boundaries. All you have to do is make a few simple changes to the words you say. That's all there is to it.

You might think that the most important communications skill is persuading people to see your point of view, but you would be wrong. As you go further down this path, you will learn that the most important skill is learning how to speak to another person's hopes, dreams, and interests, even in really difficult situations. Doing this is a matter of procedural skills that you can learn and practice, and once they become a habit, a brand new relationship with the people around you is yours for life. Now, let's start looking in detail at the mechanics of effective, painless dialogue.

CHAPTER 2

How to Have Painless Conversations: The CANDID Approach

L et's take a survey: Talk with any ten people you know, and ask them what they would say to someone who is doing something really stupid.

Even though I don't know your ten friends, I suspect that I already know the results of your survey. (And by the way, if you don't have ten friends, you've come to the right book!) Unless your friends are exceptionally gifted in dealing with people, at least eight or nine of these people will probably reply by saying something to the effect of: "You are doing something really stupid."

Let's switch places. Has anyone ever told you that *you* were doing something really stupid? Good! Now, I'd like you to tell me which sentence below would have best characterized your raw, unvarnished, private emotional reaction to this feedback:

(a) I am so thankful to be corrected about this.
(b) I am really motivated to improve my behavior in the future.
(c) I am glad that this person is taking an interest in my success.
(d) This person criticizing me is a jerk!

Let me guess. The answer was (d), right? Right. And the reason you reacted that way probably had very little to do with the actual situation, and a lot to do with how we are biologically programmed to react to threats. According to psychologists, we all have an innate survival instinct that kicks in when we are threatened by anything—and in this case, our minds do not differentiate very well between a hungry saber-toothed tiger or a manager in a neatly tailored business suit. In both cases, we instinctively jump to defend ourselves, no matter how "right" the other person is.

So this leads us to a conundrum: how do we ever successfully raise difficult subjects with people, when we are all so uniquely programmed to not like hearing them? In other words, how do you tell someone that they are doing something stupid, without ever using the word "stupid" in the sentence?

The answer is simple, but not necessarily easy. We must somehow remove the threat stimulus that causes people to resist us, while still getting our message heard and acted on. But instead of doing this, most of us operate under the misconception that we have just two stark choices in this situation:

1. To simply let it all hang out and criticize someone.
2. To avoid directly mentioning the situation at hand, either by letting it slide entirely, sugarcoating it, or resorting to euphemisms.

As we discussed in the previous chapter, both of these approaches spring from the classic *deficit-based* approach to communications—in other words, you see something wrong and try to correct it. This comes so naturally to most of us that we often don't think to use a *strength-based* approach, which focuses on creating benefits for both parties in the transaction.

In this chapter, we will explore the details of an approach that allows you to say exactly what you want to say, in a way that helps motivate and influence the other person. It consists of a formal, structured process that takes the same message you intended to deliver, and phrases it using techniques that *help the other person accept your message head-on without getting defensive*. Because it makes it easier to be candid with people, we will call it the CANDID approach. Its letters break down into specific steps that you can take, in order, to create a productive dialogue:

- *Compartmentalize* the message to create a neutral opening.
- *Ask questions* based on the other person's response.
- *Normalize* the situation.
- *Discuss* the details—factually and neutrally.
- *Incentivize* the outcome.
- *Disengage* from the discussion.

This technique breaks a difficult conversation into manageable stages, each of which uses a specific approach. This process helps take the emotional sting out of your messages, so that the conversation will be more cooperative instead of confrontational. Above all, it creates a framework for truly painless dialogues that help both you *and* the other person get what you want.

THE CANDID APPROACH IN DETAIL

When people make a major motion picture, they don't just turn on the camera and let it roll. Instead, they first have a planning process known as a *storyboard*, where they sketch out the dialogue that will happen at each step of the film. Storyboards turn a potentially chaotic process into something that has logic and order so that everyone can follow a predictable step-by-step procedure.

By comparison, when most of us approach a difficult discussion, we tend to simply open our mouths and let 'er rip. We lead with what bothers us, the other person predictably challenges our negative feedback, and before you know it you have quickly moved from a dialogue to an argument, or worse, sullen withdrawal. What I want you to do is replace these emotionally charged discussions—and the knot in the pit of your stomach that goes with them—with a storyboard of your own. A process that is carefully planned in advance will dramatically lower the heat and substantially increase your chance of a successful resolution.

The CANDID approach is a series of steps that are designed to be followed in order, which will become your storyboard for making a difficult conversation painless. The next few chapters will examine each of these steps in detail, so that you will have a confident game plan for approaching any discussion. But right now, I just want to give you a broad overview of this process. Let's take a look at how these steps work.

Compartmentalize

How do you approach a sleeping lion? Very slowly, according to an old joke. You should use much the same strategy when you first approach another person in dialogue: Start slowly and purposefully from a safe place. You can think of this process as compartmentalizing your message into the parts that are safe to talk about versus the parts that are emotionally charged, and then use these safe parts to craft a neutral opening that gets you both in dialogue. For example, when someone is in conflict with their peers, you might observe her frustration and ask her how she feels about the others. This way you are maximizing your chances of a productive discussion, and yet getting its main purpose on track from the start.

I call these opening statements the Neutral Zone, because you are starting in a place where *no one gets defensive* and *no one disagrees with you*. It goes against our human nature, but will dramatically change the tone of your discussion.

Neutral opening statements may seem like the hardest thing in the world to come up with. After all, they are the words that stand between that knot in your stomach and a conversation you wish you didn't have to have. But in reality, they usually follow a consistent pattern. Here are four types of effective neutral openings that are commonly used in difficult feedback discussions:

- *Have the other person describe what happened*, particularly when something has gone wrong.
- *Ask the other person how they are doing*, particularly when you notice a change in behavior.
- *Make a neutral observation*, particularly when you notice negative dynamics between people.
- *Use the "I" technique*, where you relate things to your own behavior or observations (e.g., "I have done this too" or "I have seen lots of people do this"), particularly when someone has made a mistake.

It is equally important to know what a neutral opening is *not*. It does not beat around the bush. It does not ask the other person about the weather or the kids. And it does not gratuitously compliment the other person. All of these are very common openings, but they rarely ever work because the other person can usually see through their ulterior motives. Instead, I want you to open with a statement that leads the other person directly into dialogue about the subject at hand, but starting in a safe and comfortable place.

The next chapter will explain these four types of neutral openings in gory detail, because they are far and away the most important part of the dialogue. You have but a few critical seconds to trigger the other person's friend-versus-foe reflex in your favor, and using the words that are most likely to do this takes practice for most people. In the meantime, simply realize for now that your goal is to get the other person talking, on-topic, and feeling comfortable at the same time. Here are some examples of where we are headed:

Situation	Typical Response	The Neutral Zone
Someone yells at a customer.	"You shouldn't have treated the customer that way."	"I can tell that customer was bothering you. Tell me about it."
Someone isn't working hard enough.	"You need to pick up the pace—or else."	"How are things going for you lately?"
Someone talks too loudly and annoys other people.	"You are way too loud."	"I notice that you communicate very strongly."
Someone isn't getting along with a co-worker.	"Why can't you and Sally get along?"	"I notice an interesting dynamic between you and Sally."
Someone is despised by their staff because she always yells at them.	"You should think seriously about knocking off the Darth Vader act."	"What kinds of things frustrate you about your team?"

Perhaps the most important thing you can take away from these examples is that most of the "typical" responses are *directive* statements, such as "be nicer," "work harder," or "stop behaving this way," while most neutral responses are either *questions* or *observations.*[1]

There is powerful psychology behind compartmentalizing your message and starting it in the Neutral Zone. It is not designed to delay the inevitable discussion of a difficult issue; rather, it engages the other person and sets the stage for the hard work that follows. More often than not, your first impression will govern the tone of the entire discussion, which means that *a good neutral opening is often all you need to lay the groundwork for a successful encounter.*

Ask Questions

Now that you have successfully started a feedback dialogue in the Neutral Zone, what do you do next? You acknowledge the other person's response, and then *keep asking questions*, based on what this person tells you. Here are some examples:

Susan: You're right, this customer did frustrate me. He never even read the manual before he called me.
You: I see. What kind of expectations do you have for a customer in situations like that?

Jill: I didn't finish this project because I haven't been feeling very well.
You: I'm sorry to hear that, Jill. How are you feeling now?

Jack: You know, I can see why you are bringing this up. I really shouldn't have gotten so angry with Beverly.
You: But at least you are aware of it, which is a good thing. How would you handle this situation in the future?

The goal here is to be "curious, not furious." Good questions show interest in the other person, and provide a face-saving way for the other person to acknowledge their behavior in their own words. More important, they often get the other person focused on solving the problem themselves, without getting upset or defensive. Because it involves taking the other person's responses, and using them as a basis to gather more information, it is an elegant, procedural step that will eventually come naturally with practice.

Normalize

Many difficult conversations revolve around a common theme of wanting someone to stop doing a Bad Thing. So guess what the most effective way is to get the other person to talk about it? By making it not seem like such a Bad Thing.

Letting people know that their behavior happens to other people, or even to you—*even when their behavior is wrong*—moves you and the other person closer to a solution. We call this step "normalizing," because we are relating their behavior to the norms of others.

It may seem funny at first glance—particularly when someone is doing something you don't like, to make it seem common or normal. It doesn't feel quite right to most of us. But ironically, this is one of the most powerful ways to *get and keep the other person in dialogue*. Normalizing a behavior doesn't mean that you approve of it, it just means that you understand it and that it is safe to talk about it—which paradoxically is more likely to lead to behavioral change. Compare these two exchanges:

Not so good:

> **ALLISON:** I couldn't help being late today. My car acted up.
> **YOU:** This is the fourth time you've been late this month!

Better:

> **ALLISON:** I couldn't help being late today. My car acted up.
> **YOU:** It is always frustrating to have your car break down on the way to work.

Do you see the difference? In the second exchange, you are *not* telling the other person that it is OK to be late to work. You are still eventually going to get to the fact that this is the fourth time that they are late, and are in fact subject to disciplinary action at this point; we'll cover that a little later in this chapter. But you aren't going to say it *quite yet*, because right now your goal is to get the other person engaged in a problem-solving dialogue rather than an unproductive session of covering their derriere.

Think carefully about all of the times that you have started a discussion by criticizing another person. Did they respond by saying, "Wow, you are so right!"? I didn't think so. That's why, as counterintuitive as it sounds, whether you discuss things in terms of how common they are, frame them in terms of your own experience, or simply acknowledge and validate the world in terms of the way the other person sees it, normalizing is one of the most powerful tools for staying in dialogue. It's also the one that perhaps goes the most against our human nature. We simply are not programmed to make people feel better about things we disagree with. But overcoming our nature and learning to normalize the worldview of the other person will generally lead you to a surprising conclusion: They become much more open to what *you* have to say. Make it part of your conversational repertoire and you will see a very tangible difference in how your most sensitive dialogues evolve.

Discuss

Here, we get to the fun part: finally mentioning the behavior that we aren't happy about. It is important to discuss problem behaviors frankly, but note that this is the *fourth* and not the *first* step of the process. Here is how to choreograph the specifics of this discussion:

- Bring up the issue at hand, as neutrally and factually as possible.
- Make the other person part of the process of solving the issue, using phrases such as "What do you think?"
- Empathize with every response—because *feelings are never wrong.* This is *not* the same as agreeing with the other person.

For example, look at the situation we mentioned earlier, about the employee who has been late with car trouble for the fourth time:

You: Having everyone here on time is critical to our operations, and I can see that this has been a recurring issue for you. Where can we go from here on this?

At this point you have "put the snake on the table," as they say in Oklahoma. You are now hitting the issue right between the eyes, in what should now be a productive dialogue.

But you have also done two other very important things here. First, you have sucked all of the emotion out of what could easily be a very emotional discussion. You are talking about facts and only facts at this point. You are not ascribing motives to the other person, you are saying nothing about this person's personality or moral character, and you are not fixing the blame. You are instead trying to fix the problem.

Some people might ask, "But what if this is an emotional situation? What if I or other people are feeling a lot of frustration toward this person?" The answer is that you will discuss this head on—but in his case, your feelings will become your facts. It is OK that something bothers you, or that another person's behavior is affecting the morale of your team, for example. What you will not do is blame, criticize, or characterize the person you are speaking with. Your mantra here should be, "Just the facts."

Second, you are not telling the other person what to do. You are *asking* them what to do. You are taking a difficult situation, gift-wrapping it, and handing it to *them* to solve. In a world where human nature leads most of us to vent our frustrations, and tell people exactly what they need to do about them, you are instead sending a powerful gesture of both respect and responsibility. It is here, in this space, that you start to sow the seeds of possible behavior change.

This step speaks to the essence of the CANDID process. You are being candid, and yet at the same time very productive. After starting in a safe place, asking questions, and validating the other person's view of the world, you are now in a position where you can painlessly talk to someone about anything and try to move it toward a solution. It is here, when you have laid the proper groundwork, that you can truly tell anyone anything.

Incentivize

Here, we get to the most important part of the process: giving the other person a *benefit* for changing, by wording things in their interest and expressing confidence in them. This simple but critical step ultimately determines how successful you will be in reaching the goals of your discussion. At the end of the day, *no one ever changes their behavior unless it benefits them in some tangible way.*

Let's expand on one of our earlier examples. Suppose that you have a manager who is a talented administrator, but all of his staff detest him because he constantly criticizes them and puts them down. First, let's try it without the incentive:

> **You:** You criticize your staff too much.
> **Van:** But I need to hold these people accountable!
> **You:** But your staff doesn't like working for you!
> **Van:** That's because they are a bunch of slackers, and I actually want them to work!

See where this is going? Absolutely nowhere, and fast. Both parties are continuing to talk past each other, as they try to dig their heels in and convince the other person they are "right." So now, let's try it again by putting benefits front and center:

> **You:** What frustrates you the most about your staff?
> **Van:** They are a bunch of whiners who don't work!
> **You:** That does sound really frustrating. Situations like that often make managers feel upset and powerless. If you'd like, I can share some communications techniques that might help you get more work out of these people.
> **Van:** OK, I'm all ears.
> **You:** (Start coaching on productive ways to speak to your employees.)

Notice a difference here? Actually there are two differences. First, the other person isn't arguing with you. (Who can argue with someone who understands you, and is offering to help?) Second, because you focus on *benefits*, they are much more open to the possibility of changing their behavior.

Even when someone is quote-unquote "in trouble," you can still word things to their benefit. Let's return to the case we discussed earlier, with the person who has been late for work four times in the last month:

Not so good:

> **You:** This is the fourth time you've been late, and you're in a lot of trouble.

Better—with incentives:

> **You:** I want you to keep being a key employee here. Even though we have a formal process for documenting being late after this many times, and I am going to write this up, I'd like to strategize how we can keep this from happening again.

People respond much better when they have an incentive for doing so, whether it is a direct benefit or the avoidance of negative consequences. Either way, by finding and selling these benefits, you provide the means to bring a feedback discussion to a productive and successful close.

Disengage

An important but often overlooked part of the conversation process is to reinforce a positive working relationship—at the close of a sensitive dialogue—by *disengaging from the discussion* and *shifting back into the normal workday.*

This step, simply put, is a matter of changing the subject toward other areas—preferably strengths—that are part of the relationship you have with this person. It can be about other work issues, or even last night's football game, so long as it represents a positive, supportive transition away from the coaching discussion.

People don't realize that after a dialogue concludes, they don't have to keep talking about the situation. (When you were a child, and your parents corrected you, how long did you want to stay on the subject?) Transitioning away from the subject at hand represents a very effective and necessary process that helps the other person feel better, while allowing them to learn—in their own time and space—from what has transpired.

PUTTING IT IN PRACTICE: A REAL-WORLD EXAMPLE

Suppose that you manage a call center that handles customer problems. Your clients expect you to log the results of each call, but one of your employees, Steve, often doesn't bother doing it. Without using a structured process to discuss this, it can become all too easy for human nature to take over, and the employee to get defensive:

> **You:** Steve, I notice that you are not following our procedures lately.
> **Steve:** It's not my fault. I can explain. We've been very busy, and I've been getting some really difficult customers . . .

Now let's try this again using the CANDID approach. Here are some of the things you can say in this situation:

Compartmentalize

> **You:** Hi, Steve. I was just looking over your logs, and was wondering if you could walk me through what happens when you get a customer call.
> **Steve:** Well, first of all, I try to make the customer happy. I know we're supposed to then create a detailed log of the call, but frankly, when it gets busy around here, it's hard for me to keep up with that.

Ask Questions

> **You:** I'm glad you're thinking of the customer first. Do you find it difficult to transcribe what happened afterwards, or are you feeling pressured to take the next call?
> **Steve:** Well, to be totally honest with you, I love working with people, and hate getting bogged down in stupid details like this.

Normalize

> **You:** I understand. Lots of bright people hate doing paperwork when they get flooded with customer calls.

Discuss

> **You:** Steve, one of the challenges of an operation like this is that our clients rate our calls on how well we document what their customers call about. In fact, this actually affects our financial performance. Is there anything that would help make it easier to keep up with these logs?
> **Steve:** You are raising a good point. I certainly don't want to make the company look bad. I can make sure these calls get logged before I take the next call.

Incentivize

> **You:** I really like the job you do here, so I want to make sure that you get the same good ratings as the rest of us.
> **Steve:** Thank you, I appreciate being here.

Disengage

> **You:** That's great. I know that you are very conscientious about your work in general, and I do appreciate how well you take care of the customers. So, how is everything else going for you these days?

By using the CANDID approach, you accomplish three important things:

- You focus on situations rather than personality, in a positive, blame-free environment.
- You give the other person an opportunity to respond professionally instead of emotionally.
- You are more likely to promote good feelings and cooperation, instead of defensiveness and confrontation.

Why "Sandwiches" Are for Lunch

Some people advocate using the "sandwich" approach of praising someone first, then mentioning the thing that bothers them, then finally praising the other person again—in other words, creating a "sandwich" of good things around the "meat" of the problem behavior.

The sandwich approach sounds good in theory. In practice, however, it often comes out like this:

"You're doing a great job, Jones. But this is the third straight month that you have missed your sales quota, and if it happens again, I'm going to have to fire you. By the way, I like your tie."

People mistakenly think that people react only to circumstances. But they really react to the way these circumstances are communicated. Every day, professionals such as police officers and health care personnel handle difficult situations professionally, by using a similar structured process. In your own workplace, you too will find these techniques to be an important part of your professional toolkit.

The problem with the sandwich approach is that, in its most basic form, it teaches you nothing about how to talk effectively about that noxious stuff in the middle of the sandwich. And just like bad meat can ruin a sandwich, a poorly-worded concern will not only put the other person on the defensive, but will often make the other more positive statements sound forced and insincere.

A tell-tale sign of a poorly-made sandwich is the word "but." If you are about to say something along the lines of "I am happy about X, *but* I am not happy about Y," save your carfare. In all likelihood, you are setting yourself up for failure.

Of course, the more general goal of connecting with someone before you correct them is a very good thing, as long as it is part of a structured process that ultimately benefits them. That is the beauty of the CANDID approach: It provides a framework that lets you get difficult messages across candidly, but at the same time much more painlessly. So now let's try the example that we just mentioned, but do it CANDID-ly:

Compartmentalize: Mentally divide the problem into its "safe" and "un-safe" components. In this case, how things are going for Jones, and what factors might be holding up his sales, are probably safer places to start than his missing the quota.

Ask questions: "Are there any issues lately that are making it harder to close your sales these days?" And depending upon how you read the situation, you might also be asking other questions such as: "How are things going on the job for you overall?", "How are you feeling about work these days?", or other areas that might be behind his performance.

Normalize: "You mentioned that it is hard to balance prospecting for new business with servicing your existing clients, and I realize that it's sometimes a real challenge for people to juggle both of these priorities."

Discuss: "We are in a situation where your sales figures directly impact our division's quarterly revenue, and everyone is being held accountable to make their quotas. Where can we go from here on this?"

Incentivize: "I know that you're a very hard worker. I would like to see you be successful here for a long time, and want to make sure that nothing stands in the way of that."

Disengage: "I really appreciate your cooperation. By the way, how are things going on the Smith account?"

Let's compare these phrases with the "sandwich" mentioned above. Do you see any differences? How would you feel hearing each of these approaches if your behavior was involved? By using the CANDID approach—which may take a little more planning and rehearsal at first but will become natural with time and practice—you will find that people are suddenly listening to you, and respecting you, like they never have before.

THE IMPORTANCE OF BEING CANDID

The art of having difficult conversations has evolved considerably over time, from simply telling people what is wrong (often leading to conflict), to "politely" telling people what is wrong (still often leading to conflict), to a much more structured process that engages the other person and speaks to their interests. In the process, we have continued to move ever closer to the true, intended purpose of dialogue: a productive, rational process designed to improve a situation for both parties.

By using the CANDID approach, you accomplish three important goals:

1. You turn difficult conversations into a painless process that is more comfortable for you to deliver.
2. You transform your relationships with other people into positive and constructive ones.
3. Most important, you gain the power to create real changes in other people by turning your focus from challenging people to helping them.

Above all, you now have the ability to replace that gnawing feeling in the pit of your stomach with a specific, procedural approach that works. So the next time you need to have an important discussion about a sensitive subject, take out a sheet of paper first and write it out: C-A-N-D-I-D. (Or better yet, use the worksheet featured in Appendix A of this book.) Then break down that difficult conversation into its component parts by writing down what you would say at each step, how the other person might respond, and how you would follow up. Plan your next feedback dialogue on paper, then try it out in real life and you will see for yourself. There is a process behind the mechanics of influencing people to change their performance and behavior, and it really works.

When you use this technique in your own daily interactions with others, you are tapping in to one of the most powerful forces in human behavior: another person's own self-interest. We hate being criticized and being told what to do, but we love learning new skills and being helped. When you learn to make this distinction, and put it into practice in your own life, you will soon learn that it does much more than make for painless conversations: It changes everything about the relationship between you and the people around you.

So are you now ready to go out and start turning your most challenging interactions with people into positive, strength-based dialogues? Not quite yet. The steps of the CANDID process are logical and rational, but they all have one thing in common: Every single one runs counter to what most of us have been saying most of our lives, and the pull of human nature is incredibly strong. So read on, and start learning over the next few chapters how to make each of these steps come alive in your own most sensitive discussions, and do it with a pen and paper in hand. In just a few short pages, you will begin opening the door to a whole new world of engaging and influencing other people. Enjoy the ride.

NOTE

1. This approach borrows from what the great psychologist Carl Rogers referred to as "unconditional positive regard," where you foster an open and accepting dialogue that makes it easier for the other person to open up and speak with you.

The CANDID Approach in Detail

CHAPTER 3

Compartmentalize Your Message: The Neutral Zone

Compartmentalizing your message doesn't just focus on what you say. Instead, it involves taking the issue you want to deal with, unpacking and spreading it out in front of you, separating it into its safe and unsafe parts, and only then, creating a neutral opening that will get you into dialogue with the other person. You do it with a pencil and paper, and not with your emotions. It is a very different and very effective way of looking at a difficult conversation with someone. Let's break down the mechanics of how it works.

STEP 1: UNPACKING THE DIALOGUE

Let's take an example. You work in a machine shop, and everyone works hard and does their share—except for Slowpoke Smith off in the back corner. He is, at best, half as productive as everyone else. He's been there for a long time, back before people started measuring productivity in any kind of meaningful way. He has lots of great war stories and is "one of the guys," but he drags down the performance of the whole shop.

First, let's look at how most people would probably approach this dialogue. They would probably start by telling ol' Slowpoke that he needs to pick up the pace. Or perhaps that he needs to pick up the pace *or else*. While I am not particularly clairvoyant, I'll bet that I can predict his responses.

- "I've been doing this since before you were born."
- "It's the fault of these dadgum new machines. They are too complicated."

- "This used to be a nice place to work, but ever since you started managing us, you want to squeeze every penny of extra profit out of us. We're just like your equipment."
- "I'm interested in quality, not quantity."
- "The only time you pay any attention to us old timers is to hassle us to do more work."

Meanwhile, the one thing you were hoping he would say—namely, "Golly, I should start working harder"—somehow never makes it into the conversation. And far too often, this kind of stalemate continues until you give up or he gets fired.

Now let's try a different approach. Take the whole issue, unpack it into its component parts, and lay it all out in front of you. Take your time and think through all of the facets of it, from both your perspective and his. Most important, have a pencil (or a word processor) in hand when you do this, and don't hold back on writing down anything that comes to mind. Start with what you think about the other person, his good and bad points in this situation, and where his interests are. If you do that in the case we just described above, here are some of the things that might end up on your sheet:

- He is slow.
- He has been here for a long time.
- He did not like the new machines we installed.
- He will be retiring in a few years.
- He likes to socialize rather than work.
- He files union grievances at the drop of a hat.
- He has had some good ideas for making products better.
- His quality is good overall.
- His co-workers are frustrated because they feel we let him get away with goofing off.
- He is proud of what he does for a living.

Don't stop there. Now look in the mirror, think about how *you* feel, and keep writing. Some of the things that might end up on your sheet about yourself might include the following:

- I am concerned about productivity. Competitors are always squeezing our margins.

- I am concerned about morale and turnover.
- Sometimes I push too hard on people, and don't get the results I want.
- I don't just want to make a buck, I want this place to be a good job for everyone.
- I don't like to play favorites.

By now, you should hopefully have a pretty good list. More important, you have a pretty good overview of how both of you might see this situation. Now, go down this list and decide which things are safe to talk about, and which things are not.

Slowpoke's tenure? That's pretty safe. He is very proud of that. And his quality is something he takes a lot of pride in as well. His productivity? That isn't quite so safe. And the way other co-workers see him? That probably isn't safe at all.

Now, how about you? Your concerns about morale and a good working environment are pretty safe because they are ultimately in Slowpoke's interest. Ditto being fair to everyone. On the other hand, your concerns about profitability are a gray area. You could unpack that a little further into a concern about making sure people keep their jobs, which is safe, and a concern for making more profit, which may not be so safe, particularly among employees who feel they are being pressured to work harder.

So what first seemed like a very difficult problem—namely, trying to get a crotchety old timer to pick up his pace—suddenly has all sorts of safe places to start. And more important, lots of unsafe places to avoid. You can see very clearly, in black and white, what kinds if issues will get Smith talking, and above all, which ones will *not*.

Now here is the punchline to this exercise: Yes, you are going to eventually talk about the unsafe parts of this situation. You simply aren't going to discuss them *first*. Unlike most people, you will focus on the safe parts first and the unsafe parts later. We'll discuss that step in the process in a later chapter, but for now, compare these two opening statements.

How most people start the conversation:

"Gee, Smith, you are really slow and always talking with people. We need you to work harder and save your socializing for after hours."

How you will start the conversation, in a safe place:

> "You've been doing this for a long time, and your quality is better than a lot of people. Could you walk me through the process you use when you manufacture a new tool?"

Do you notice a difference between how Smith will probably respond to these two statements? And more important, is there a difference to how *you* feel? Does a scary conversation suddenly seem a little less scary? Good. This is exactly what we want to see.

No matter what it is, *every* situation has safe and unsafe parts. The safe parts are those areas of interest and agreement for the other person, while the unsafe parts are clearly areas of criticism or disagreement. The following ideas will help you start thinking about these safe parts.

1. Does the other person have an agenda that relates to the issue? For example, when someone is difficult to work with, she may be highly invested in her way of doing things. Similarly, someone who dresses poorly may have strong ideas about being more casual in a work setting. In both cases, discussing how *they* feel about things may represent a safe place to start.

2. How does the other person feel about the situation? For example, if the other person is in conflict with someone, *his* side of the story is probably far and away the safest part of the dialogue. Likewise, if another person disagrees with you, she will usually be more than happy to share more details about why she feels that way.

3. What motivates the other person? Suppose that someone couldn't care less about how he is doing his job. A discussion about the potential to earn more money, feel more secure in their position, or a question about how they are doing in general, might be a better place to start thinking about this issue. Conversely, when someone puts a great deal of emphasis on personal or career success, this could be an appropriate lead-in for discussing behaviors that are keeping her from reaching her potential.

4. What things are sources of pride for the other person? When things make other people proud of themselves, they can be a great place to start provided they relate to the issue at hand. For example, someone who has a problem with anger may also be proud of his intensity, while someone who is slow and plodding may value her attention to detail. We will devote a whole chapter later to the subject of *reframing* people's behaviors, but for now, ask yourself what the other person values about him- or herself.

5. Are there "hot buttons" you should avoid? "Don't talk to her about that" is often a code phrase for situations where trying to discuss a specific issue leads to hostility and defensiveness. I would like to reframe this as a situation where no one has yet had a *safe* discussion about this issue with this person, one that ultimately speaks to her interests as well as everyone else's. So hold the thought for now that you may yet be able to have a productive, neutral, factual discussion on this issue, as long as you do not start out by pressing a hot button.

Even really bad situations have safe places to start the dialogue. For example, hopefully you never have to question someone who has been arrested for a crime, but good police officers will tell you that an effective formal interrogation often starts with understanding what is going on in the other person's head and then speaking to it. For example, instead of focusing on the crime first, the officer might begin by asking the person in custody if things have been tough for him lately. This may feel funny or even wrong to some people (after all, this person is a suspected criminal under arrest) but the question is, is your objective to get them talking or make them clam up and get defensive?

In general, it does feel funny to speak to another person's agenda, but as we walk through the process of managing a difficult dialogue, you will learn that it gives you *more* power, *more* influence, and *less* resistance than the old, blunt, painful way of giving feedback. This is why you need to start ignoring that little voice that tells you that speaking to another person's interests equates to being soft, and start learning where these safe places will lead you in the overall course of the discussion.

Perhaps the most important thing about these safe places is that they come from the situation itself—which means that you can use them to get into dialogue right away about this situation, which in turn is a key goal of a painless discussion. When faced with an uncomfortable subject, the majority of us either blurt out our concerns, or we decide to start the discussion with something "nice" to say: We talk about the weather, ask the other person about their kids, or compliment them about their work.

I don't want you to beat around the bush like this, for two very important reasons. First, the other person will often sense your discomfort and see through your "nice" intro, leaving you with the worst of both worlds: She will start to feel defensive, and yet have no idea what you are about to say. Second, once you snap the other person back to reality by shifting to an unpleasant topic, you are often poisoning the well for future casual dialogue, by setting up an expectation in the other person that a "yeah, but" may be lurking in the background.

This is why I want you to start your discussion totally on topic, and stay there until it reaches a conclusion. I want you to be honest, authentic, and yet aware of the other person's thoughts, feelings, hopes, and dreams at the same time. Above all, I want you to get comfortable with the idea that even the most sensitive subjects have a place where you can both agree to start talking.

Now, let's look at how you work the safe parts of this problem in a neutral opening that comfortably gets you both into dialogue.

STEP 2: CREATING A NEUTRAL OPENING

Let's recap. So far, you have examined the situation, ideally with a pen or keyboard in hand. You have broken it down into the parts that are safe and unsafe to talk about. The one thing you haven't done yet is open your mouth. So your next step from here is to take these safe things and use them to form an opening statement to the other person that I call the Neutral Zone.

Once you have established what things are safe and unsafe to talk about, creating the Neutral Zone can actually be a surprisingly straightforward process. This is because while there are more different kinds of situations with people than most of us could count, there are a limited number of ways to safely engage people on any of these topics. As we mentioned in the previous chapter, we could boil down the mechanics of a good neutral opening into one of four basic forms:

1. Ask the other person to describe what happened.
2. Ask the other person how he or she is doing.

3. Make a neutral observation.
4. Use the "I" technique.

In each of these cases, you take the safe things that you have identified from examining the situation and adapt them to one of these four types of neutral openings. Let's look at each of them in detail.

Have the Other Person Describe What Happened

The game is tied with seconds left. Your star basketball player is at the foul line. She shoots her first foul shot and it bounces off the rim. Looking more determined, she heaves the ball toward the basket one more time—and this time it isn't even close. The other team high-fives each other as time runs out and they win the contest.

It is this woman's job to sink baskets when the game is on the line. It didn't happen this time. Perhaps it hasn't happened other times as well. What do you say to her when you meet in the locker room the next day?

As an untrained observer, you might focus on how she failed. If you were being nice about it, perhaps you might ask the player what went wrong. If you weren't being nice, you might point out that her spot on the team is at risk. Either way, you have just changed the dynamics of the discussion to one where the player is defending herself. But I suspect what you really want to do here is troubleshoot the problem and hopefully fix it.

This is why, when something goes wrong, far and away the best neutral opening is to ask the other person to describe what happened—neutrally, factually, and without blame. For example, my opening statement to this player might be something along the lines of, "I'm sure you feel bad about those last couple of shots last night. Walk me through what was happening up there on the foul line." Instead of a threatening confrontation, you now have offered an open invitation to talk. More important, you now have your very best chance to gather information to help you both fix the problem.

With a typical critical "what's wrong" kind of opening, you can almost always expect a response focused on self-defense. For example, this player might respond by saying that someone else distracted her, or that the referee riled her up on the last call, or perhaps even that you put her in the game too quickly. Unless she has a superhuman level of maturity, she is much more likely to blame what happened on the phase of the moon than on herself.

Now let's try my approach of asking her to break down the mechanics of what happened in the game. We might get a very different set of responses, such as one of the following:

> "My shots were about six inches off to the left of where I normally sink them."
>
> "My head really wasn't in the game last night. I've been battling the flu all week."
>
> "To be honest, I tightened up because I knew the game was on the line."

In the first case, I now know that I may be dealing with a problem of technique, which we could possibly address through coaching. In the second case, the lesson might be for both of us to be frank with each other about her health status in the future. And in the third case, I now have valuable information about how she responds to pressure. In each of these cases, I am getting data that helps me as I move toward the next steps in the process of dialogue.

Conversely, if she was being criticized, nothing she would have said would be of any use to me at all. I cannot go out there and change the behavior of fans or referees, I cannot adopt fantastical restrictions on when I should put players in a game, and I can't change the phase of the moon. I can only do my very best to gather information from her, and then try and influence a positive solution.

In general, asking someone to describe the mechanics of what happened is one of the best ways to start talking about the safe parts of the discussion, particularly when someone does something wrong. Some of the situations where you might consider using this opening include the following:

- Someone makes an important mistake that they should not have.
- A person has chronic, long-term performance problems.
- The other person seems to "choke up" in critical situations.
- Things are not getting done right because people aren't communicating well.
- Someone didn't do what was expected of them.

This kind of opening works best in these situations because you have shifted the focus from a *fault-finding* mission to a *fact-finding* mission, in a way that engages the other person as a partner. Some good examples of these kinds of statements include:

"Could you walk me through how you do this?"
"When situations like this happen, how do you usually handle them?"
"It sounds like this was very frustrating for you. Tell me about it."
"What approach do you use for doing this?"
"If it were up to you, how do you think we should perform this task?"

Questions like these all have one thing in common: They assume a listening stance regarding the problem, while showing a genuine interest and respect toward the other person. Moreover, they are all "open" questions that invite dialogue, rather than "closed" questions designed to be answered with a single yes or no. The other person's responses to these questions can then, in turn, lead you toward a positive, constructive discussion aimed at the mechanics of the situation.

While asking for information is a good, general-purpose safe opening for troubleshooting problems, you should also be aware of some pitfalls to avoid while using it.

1. *The Interrogation.* Asking someone about how they do things with genuine interest is generally OK, even when it is clear that you are trying to troubleshoot a problem. What is not OK are harsh, repeated questions that put the other person on the spot and on the defensive: "What did you do? When did you do it? Where were you on the night of the 23rd?" Remember that your goal is to open space for dialogue, not just pump people for information.

2. *Veiled Criticism.* There are questions, and then there are statements designed as questions. For example, watch what happens on some television talk shows when a host questions someone with an opposing view. These "questions" often take the form of "How can you justify such a stupid policy?" or "What do you have to say to this obvious failure?" These are only questions in the sense of sharing a question mark, and their goal is to express negative emotions rather than solve problems or gather information. In a similar manner, many feedback questions can turn critical if they are not prepared and asked from the right mindset.

3. *Closed Questions.* As we mentioned earlier, your opening statement should be an invitation to talk, not a collection of "yeses" and "no's."

Make sure that the form of your opening truly gives the other person an opportunity to talk frankly, and gives you an opportunity to listen and gather useful information.

Bringing these issues around to your own dialogues, remember that you are often feeling upset or angry about the situation that led to this conversation, so be careful that these emotions do not leak into the content of your questions. This is one reason why it is critically important to write down both your thoughts and your possible openings, so you can see and evaluate them in black and white. When you see statements like, "Is this really the way you wanted to do this?" instead of, "Tell me how you do this," keep workshopping your opening until it becomes more likely to get the other person talking.

This having been said, the very functional act of asking for information is often the perfect antidote to what could become an overly emotional discussion. Try it yourself in situations like these, and watch more people start opening up and talking with you.

Ask the Other Person How He or She Is Doing

Picture this: You have a co-worker who has been your best friend at work for years. She works hard, is unfailingly pleasant, and has always had your back. The two of you have always been a great team, and she is one of the reasons you look forward to coming to work in the morning.

But recently, something has changed. This past month, she has seemed vaguely angry all the time. Work that used to get turned around quickly has been piling up on her desk. Worst of all, she has become unpleasant and critical about everything you do.

Finally, you decide to do something about it. You screw up the courage to walk in to her cubicle and start telling her how disappointed you are in her. You tell her that you are tired of her constant backbiting and criticism. Finally, you point out that she used to be one of the hardest workers on the team, but that nowadays it seems like everyone else is covering for her.

She takes a deep breath, stares back at you, and says, "My son was just diagnosed with cancer three weeks ago."

People are not constant. Nor are they made of steel. Things change over time, and often what you see on the surface is just the tip of another person's iceberg. And yet we often respond instinctively to what we see, with the result that we start many of our most difficult conversations by missing the point of them entirely. This is why one of the best places to start a dialogue, particularly when something changes, is to simply ask the other person how he or she is doing. Doing so could uncover any of a host of previously unspoken issues:

- There may be factors to the situation you don't know about.
- There may be serious personal issues going on in this person's life.
- This person may be upset with you, but too proud or too angry to have said anything.
- There may be conflicts between this person and his or her teammates.
- This person may be burning out at what he or she is doing and need a change.

Or there may be nothing "wrong" at all except for this person's performance change. Baseball players do not always perform the same at age 42 as they did at age 22, factory workers may not be able to lift 100 pounds of equipment like they once used to, and people from all walks of life can lose their touch, temporarily or permanently. And even when you are at the top of your game, people are human, make mistakes, and have down times. When you ask someone about their current situation, you gather the information you need to know whether you are walking in to a performance discussion or a life situation.

This type of opening is most effective when you are trying to address ongoing performance problems, particularly when something has changed. It works because you are showing concern for the other person while gathering information that helps you understand and troubleshoot the problem. It can help replace excuses or defensiveness with information of which you may not have been aware, information that can help you focus on a more productive, solution-oriented discussion.

One caveat, however: Of all of the four neutral openings we discuss here, this is one that may *not* always be a good idea to use. Why? Asking someone how they are doing is a very relationship-oriented question, and the appropriateness of this question depends on the context of that relationship. For example:

- If you don't have an ongoing relationship with someone, barging in and asking, "How are you doing?" may seem inappropriately personal.
- If you are a manager who normally remains aloof from your subordinates, asking an employee, "How are you doing?" may sound like a leading question that comes across as threatening. (For example, one

of my seminar attendees reported that when her boss said this, she replied, "I thought I was fine until you came in. What did I do wrong?")

- When someone sees you as an adversary or a competitor, asking, "How are you doing?" may possibly be greeted with, "None of your #$%& business!"

Taking things a step further, asking how someone is doing must come across as an invitation, not an interrogation—and particularly in the workplace, it is inappropriate to go beyond this expression of concern and ask people prying questions about their personal lives. When you ask how someone is doing, keep a respectful distance, and be aware that some people may prefer not to disclose how they are doing or feeling to you. The guarded response "I'm fine" sometimes speaks as loudly as a raft of details.

That said, when you ask someone how things are going for them, you are generally miles ahead of the way most people discuss changes in performance—namely, criticism or interrogations that often lead to defensiveness and hostility. It is part of a larger mindset that seeks to learn from people rather than simply barking orders. Done well, it can also show a level of concern for others that builds and strengthens your relationships with them.

Make a Neutral Observation

When you are hoping to accomplish a behavioral change in another person—for example, if someone talks too much or creates too much negativity—starting a conversation with observational phrases such as "I notice . . ." or "It seems like . . ." can often engage the other person in productive dialogue, *as long as what you are noticing is neutral and nonjudgmental*.

Observations like these should always focus on *facts, not feelings*. Done correctly, they should open up a dialogue from a position of mutual respect. So, for example, you cannot say, "I notice that you are acting like a jerk"—which is both personal and threatening—but you *can* say, "I notice that you get frustrated when people need your time." This latter statement is a factual observation that doesn't challenge the other person, which, in turn, will often get the other person into a productive dialogue about why they are in fact acting like a jerk.

Above all, remember that you are still in the Neutral Zone at this point, and in general that means that this isn't the right time to make an observation about the problem itself. Instead, your job is to make a *neutral* observation, for the express purpose of engaging the other person in dialogue without putting him on the defensive. It can (and should) relate to the issue at hand, but should never tread on emotionally charged territory. Here are some good examples of neutral observations:

Blunt Observation	Neutral Observation
You talk too much.	I notice you like to be engaged with people around the office.
You smell.	I notice that some people get active and sweaty before they come to work.
You are a meanie with no social graces.	I notice that people sometimes get on your nerves.
You are a salesperson who couldn't sell to save your life.	It seems like it's hard to get sales prospects to respond these days. That must be really frustrating.

While neutral observations can be useful for many kinds of situations, they are absolutely tailor made for those occasions when someone is in conflict with others. Do you have to deal with people who are rude, yell at coworkers or customers, or are difficult to work with? Good, because believe it or not, these people are actually much *easier* to get into dialogue with than most people. Why? Because they are candidates for what I call the *perfect neutral opening*.

The perfect neutral opening involves taking an observation about people's behavior, thinking through how *they* see it, and then simply putting it in the form of a question. In layman's terms, this usually means asking them what bugs them about other people. Here are some examples:

"What frustrates you about working with José?"
"I notice that my team seems to get under your skin a lot. What kinds of things bother you about them?"
"What kinds of things could your coworkers be doing to treat you better?"

I call this the *perfect neutral opening* because it is almost guaranteed to get the other person talking to you, without ever putting them on the defensive.

People usually *love* to discuss their grievances with other people. And this is actually a great thing because you are now exactly where you want to be: in dialogue about the situation.

From your end, the perfect neutral opening probably feels a little like driving north to go south. You really want to talk about the *other* person's behavior, right? You want to get to how they are too mean, too angry, too thin-skinned, or whatever. And perhaps you think the other people are just fine, thank you. Every fiber of your being wants to call out angry or difficult people and show them the error of their ways.

The problem is, they don't see themselves the way you see them. In his classic book *How to Win Friends and Influence People*, Dale Carnegie famously pointed out how gangsters of his era saw themselves as benign figures who were good at heart, and what he had to say in 1936 is, if anything, even more true in the new millennium.[1] As much as you might love to enlighten people about how they come across to others, you can't start there unless you want them to push back, defend themselves, blame others, and above all tune you out.

By comparison, what the perfect neutral opening does is get you talking about what sets people off. This gives you a golden opportunity to acknowledge, validate, and normalize everything they tell you, as we will discuss further in the next chapter. And finally, you will leverage all of this to explore ways for the other person to handle these situations more productively and be less frustrated, to the benefit of all concerned.

Use the "I" Technique

I sometimes introduce this technique to audiences, with my tongue firmly in cheek, by calling it "how to tell someone they are stupid without ever using the word stupid in the sentence."

Of course, I do not believe in calling anyone stupid; rather, my intention is to find a humane and painless way to talk about what happens when someone does something that was ill-considered or ill-advised, with the help of a little principle from behavioral psychology known as *modeling*.

People do not learn most things from scratch. Instead, we learn by observing the behavior of other people, particularly when they make mistakes. When we tell people that they have done something wrong, it usually kicks in a powerful survival urge to defend themselves, but when we instead show them an example of someone else making the same mistake, they tend to learn from it and not get defensive.

So who can we predictably use to "model" poor choices as a learning tool? Why, ourselves, of course. And using this tool could not be easier. Simply take "you" statements about a problem, and replace them with "I" statements about your own experiences. In its basic form, using the "I" technique involves replacing "You made a mistake" with "I have made mistakes like this, and here is what happened."

By using this technique to share our own foibles with other people, we create both a learning experience and a bond of fellowship. Compare these examples and see what we mean:

Not so good: "You shouldn't have pressed that button."
Better: "The last time I pressed that button, it brought things to a halt."

Not so good: "You should have made a backup before your computer crashed."
Better: "I get frustrated when I forget to make a backup and lose my work, so I know how you feel."

Not so good: "That wasn't the most appropriate thing to say to the boss."
Better: "I hate it when I say things like that to my manager, and it doesn't go over well."

The "I" technique is a remarkably effective way of normalizing behavior when you open a discussion because you are correcting them without criticizing them. Who can argue with the fact that *you* have done something stupid? By making it all about you, in a very real sense you are making it all about them.

This leads to an interesting corollary. What do you say when you haven't shared the other person's experience? Or when someone does something so profoundly, incredibly stupid that you could never own up to it with a straight face? The good news is that you can still use the "I" technique very effectively in situations like these, by talking about what you have observed in *other people*. For example:

- "I have seen lots of other people do this."
- "This is a very common error that people often make."
- "I've seen this happen before."

I Understand That You Are in Handcuffs

A good friend of mine was a police officer for many years, and I have always been impressed by her stories of how good cops communicate in difficult situations. One that completely took me by surprise was the following: What are officers trained to say to someone who is in handcuffs in the back of their police cruiser, on the long ride back to the police station?

If you have watched too many cop shows on television, you might expect that they say something like "We've got you now, you dirty rat." In reality, they use the observational "I" technique to lower the heat of the situation, saying things like:

- "You aren't the first person to be in this situation."
- "Lots of people get caught doing something stupid like this. If you learn from it, it's going to be OK."
- "You have lots of company. We are probably arresting a dozen people for the same thing tonight."

Why are cops trained to turn on the empathy at times like this? For one simple reason: It keeps them safe. There are few more dangerous moments in police work than when someone is in custody who really, really does not want to be there. Making someone feel less guilty can prevent a confrontation from happening in the first place. This is why the "I" technique is so powerful, even in very critical situations.

I call this the observational "I" technique because instead of talking about yourself, you are talking about your observations of others. Either way, you are shifting the focus off of another person's mistakes and putting it on human nature in a way that opens the door to safe and productive dialogue.

In either its regular or observational forms, what you are accomplishing with the "I" technique is a form of *normalizing* a situation, or making it appear more normal, a technique we will discuss in further detail in Chapter 5. It is a remarkably effective way of draining the guilt out of a situation to create better feelings on both sides. In the process, you are creating an environment where people can safely and honestly talk with you about any situation, even when they are at fault.

FINDING THE NEUTRAL ZONE TAKES PRACTICE

Finding a Neutral Zone to start from is often the hardest part of a conversation because every fiber of your body wants to simply lead with the thing we are upset about. This is why most of us cannot do it on the fly. Instead, we must prepare and rehearse what we are going to say first, preferably in writing. With time and practice, the art of finding the Neutral Zone will eventually become natural, but for almost all of us it is a learned skill.

Creating a neutral opening is a procedural skill, but the results of it are filtered through your physical and emotional presence. So take the techniques shown here, write down how they apply to your situation, and then practice what you are going to say aloud. Delivered with genuine empathy and concern for the other person, these openings set the stage for engaging people further in dialogue through appropriate questions, acknowledgment and validation, emotion-free logic, and benefits—topics we will cover in the following chapters.

An important closing point about compartmentalizing your message is that it is *not* the same as sugarcoating it. Many people feel that to soften the blow of a difficult discussion, they should say nice things about the other person or make the situation sound less serious than it is. By comparison, compartmentalizing the issue and creating a Neutral Zone keeps the focus squarely on the issue at hand, in a way that engages the other person in dialogue without the need to minimize or distract from the issue and its importance. In the process, you create a tone of respect that sets the stage for the entire dialogue.

NOTE

1. Dale Carnegie, *How to Win Friends and Influence People* (*Anniversary Edition*) (New York: Pocket Books, 1998).

CHAPTER 4

Ask Questions:
From Furious to Curious

S uppose you have just opened up a conversation on a difficult subject by using a skillful neutral opening. The other person has just responded. You can tell by her response that she probably does not agree with you. What happens next?

For most people, this stage of a dialogue is the moment they fear the most. Ideally, we would love it if the other person would respond to our neutral opening by saying "You are raising a really good issue. In fact, I have been thinking about my behavior in this area, and from now on I plan to (come in on time/shower more often/stop yelling at people/whatever)." The problem is they don't ever say that. So most of us get that gnawing feeling in our stomach and think, *Uh-oh, what do I say now?*

You are asking the wrong question here. Instead of worrying about what you will *say* to someone, you should be thinking about what you will *ask* them.

In this chapter, we are going to explore the liberating concept that good questions are the key to any successful discussion. This concept is a revelation for most of us because we are so inherently programmed to talk *at* people, not listen *to* them. As a result, we all fall blindly into the pothole of explaining our position, defending ourselves, or heaven forbid, criticizing the other person. And then we are off to the races, in a discussion that usually spirals downward out of our grasp.

Here we will look at the refreshing idea that you don't have to say anything in the early stages of a conversation, even in difficult situations; in fact, *particularly* in difficult situations. You simply have to take the thoughts and ideas that another person gift wraps and hands you, unwrap them, and use them to create good questions. In the process, you will painlessly and procedurally get yourself in the habit of getting people to talk, hearing their stories, and building a dialogue.

WHY THE RIGHT QUESTIONS WORK

The word "question" is derived from the Latin version of the phrase "to seek." This is also the root of the power of good questions: They seek information from other people, and the very act of seeking confers a level of interest and respect on them. Here are some of the reasons that the right questions are so powerful in a difficult discussion.

1. *Questions provide data.* Suppose that someone makes the blunt statement that she hates working on your team. It is not only painful to hear, but it also doesn't tell you very much. When you start probing what someone dislikes about her job, any of a number of paths might open up. She may dislike a particular coworker, she might feel the overtime takes her away from her kids, or she might think you demand too much. Unless you start asking questions, whatever path you take to respond to her could take you a long way in the wrong direction.

At a more subtle level, what you *don't* hear can sometimes provide as much information as what you *do* hear. When someone sidesteps an issue or acts uncomfortable talking about something, you can gain a sense of where someone might be sensitive, shy, or have strong uncomfortable feelings. This in turn can help you know where to probe gently or perhaps back off entirely. In general, good questions can often change the direction that a difficult conversation takes.

2. *Questions give the other person a voice.* In Native American culture, there is a tradition known as the "talking stick." When people are gathered in a group, individuals take turns giving each other a stick, and whoever is holding the stick is the only person allowed to speak. Everyone else is expected to listen and pay close attention to the person holding this talking stick.

When you focus on asking questions in the early stages of a discussion, you make the very powerful gesture of handing the other person the talking stick every time you open your mouth. This gesture of respect alone can carry more weight in a difficult conversation than even the questions themselves. By taking a curious rather than condemning approach, you are much more likely to foster cooperation instead of confrontation.

3. *Questions open up space in a discussion.* Left to our own devices, conversations about difficult subjects would be short and to the point. We would declare what we don't like, the other person would stop doing it, and life would continue on happily ever after.

The problem with this simple view of the world is that we are describing a monologue, not a dialogue, and monologues do not tend to be well received by the person on the other end. Most of us want to feel like we have the time and space to get our side of the story across, and questions open up space for this to happen on both sides of the transaction.

Here is an example of how good questions can totally change the dynamics of a sensitive discussion:

Not so good:

Lisa: I can explain why this project didn't get finished on time.
You: I don't really want to hear any excuses at this point. I am just upset that you missed the deadline.
Lisa (growing angry): Oh yeah, you should try dealing with what we have to, and see how well you would have done!

Better:

Lisa: I can explain why this project didn't get finished on time.
You: Sure, tell me more. What kind of challenges did you face?
Lisa: First, they changed the requirements on us midway through the project. Then Mindy got sick. And after that, people got so bogged down

with their other responsibilities that it was hard to get everyone moving forward.

You: Wow. That is a lot of things in a short time. How do you think we should proceed from here?

In the first case where a statement was used instead of a question, it had the effect of closing off space for dialogue, leading Lisa to angrily defend herself. By comparison, the questions in the second example opened up space, turning an argument into a discussion.

To the untrained ear, these two examples may seem like a simple case of being blunt versus being empathetic. They aren't. The latter case is following a procedure, and this procedure is even more critical to use when you are unhappy with the other person. Asking appropriate questions does not imply you agree with the other person, nor does it take power away from your concerns. In fact, it gives you power and credibility by following the rules of productive dialogue.

THE ANATOMY OF A GOOD QUESTION

You have probably noticed that we are frequently using the term "good question" in this chapter. There is a reason for this because the act of simply asking questions is not enough in a difficult conversation. The benefits of these questions do not simply derive from putting a question mark at the end of each sentence; they spring from respect and an invitation to dialogue.

Good Questions are Relevant and On Topic

There is a joke about people calling for help when they were stuck in an elevator and reaching a psychologist by mistake. They asked her desperately if she could do anything to help them, and flustered, she responded, "How do you feel about being stuck in an elevator?"

You do not want to come across like this psychologist in your most critical dialogues with people. Keeping the discussion focused on the subject at hand — and in particular, on the other person's responses — represents a sign of respect. In general, the best questions often follow the lead of the other person and the rhythm of the conversation. Here are some examples:

Other Person's Response	Follow-Up Question
I am struggling with this project.	What kinds of things do you feel are the most difficult?
The MIS department keeps dropping the ball on this.	What do you think the MIS department should be doing?
I just don't know what to think anymore. We don't seem to have any clear direction.	If you were the boss, what would you recommend?
I was disappointed when you criticized our work in this morning's meeting.	How would you have preferred that I handle the situation?
I feel like a failure.	What things feel like stuck points for you?

In each of these cases, these questions take the other person's statement to the next level by asking them to clarify the situation or share their preferred solution. At a more subtle level, you are also helping them to shift the focus from complaining to problem solving. Above all, you are engaging them in a dialogue that is open and nonthreatening, even in a difficult situation.

Good Questions Are Empathetic

Empathy is defined as "vicariously experiencing the feelings, thoughts, and experience of another," and it underscores a point that is perhaps the cornerstone of a difficult discussion: Feelings are never wrong.

Empathetic questions sound good on paper, but they are often the last things we think to say when we are upset with another person. This is ironically why they are so powerful. They take nothing away from the strength of our arguments; in fact, they give us strength because they take away any doubts in the other person's mind about understanding them. Here are some examples of showing empathy in the form of a question:

- Has this been difficult for you?
- Are you feeling a little frustrated?
- How do you feel about that?

- Does her behavior bother you?
- How did that affect you?

Note that the effectiveness of empathy questions is highly dependent upon the listener. Some personality types want you to care about them, while others simply want to get down to business. Probe gently for feelings in a discussion, read the body language and facial expressions, and know when to back off. That said, however, be aware that the vast majority of us show too *little* empathy in a discussion, not too much.

Good Questions Open Rather Than Close Dialogue

Do you know what is one of the worst words with which to close a question? Believe it or not, it is "you." Consider the following examples:

- I think we should do it this way, don't you?
- You could do something about this, couldn't you?
- You did take care of this, didn't you?

Ironically, while each of these phrases ends with "you," the focus is squarely on "me" because these are closed questions that leave the other person little room for dialogue. Worse, these are also presumptive questions, the only purpose of which is to confirm that the other person agrees with what you want, putting them in the awkward position of correcting you if they do not.

In general, closed questions with a "yes" or "no" answer do not contribute to your strategic purpose at this point, which is to lower the heat and draw the other person into productive dialogue. This is why you should generally use open questions that give people the time and space to construct their own authentic answer. Here is how the three questions above would work as open questions:

- How do you feel we should do it?
- Do you feel you could do something about this?
- Is this on your agenda to take care of?

Open questions stimulate dialogue, while closed questions limit it. This means that your leading questions should normally be open ones, with closed questions perhaps having a role when you need to take back control of the conversation and keep it moving. In general, most people ask many *fewer* open questions than they should in a difficult conversation.

Good Questions Paraphrase the Other Person

Paraphrasing is a technique that can supercharge the effectiveness of a good question. It involves taking the statements that another person hands you, unpacking them, and rephrasing them in your own words. Paraphrasing sends a very powerful signal to other people: It tells them that you heard them, that you understood them, that you accept what they just said as being important to them, and perhaps most of all, that it is safe to talk about what they are saying.

Paraphrasing is a central component of what psychologists call *active listening*, a process that engages the other person and builds a relationship in dialogue. Here are some examples of how it works:

> **JOE:** I wish people would just shut up and get back to work around here!
> **YOU:** So you wish that other people would stop talking and do their fair share. What do you think might help people get more focused on their jobs?

> **LUPE:** I have been late more often these days because so much has been going on in my life.
> **YOU:** It sounds like you have been juggling a lot lately. Are things feeling overwhelming for you?

> **HANS:** The problem is all Steve's fault. He's always getting on my case!
> **YOU:** Clearly Steve has been getting under your skin. What kinds of things does he do that frustrate you?

In each of these cases, the skills you use here are less about being a good conversationalist and more about being a good translator. You are interpreting what the other person says and then using this to preface a question that both shows empathy and elicits more information.

Each of these approaches serves as part of a larger whole, to engage the other person in dialogue and give their opinions importance. And ironically, they become particularly important when you are least happy with this person because good questions are generally one of your quickest ways to find points of influence and consensus. Finally, they provide an important and procedural means of staying in dialogue because they are fundamentally based around the response of the other person.

QUESTIONS TO AVOID

Questions are, of course, a double-edged sword. The right kinds of questions can show interest, understanding, and fellowship, particularly in sensitive dialogues. Conversely, the wrong questions can have exactly the opposite effect. Picture a detective thriller where the police are grilling a suspect: "What were you doing last night? What happened to the girl? Does this gun look familiar to you?" These kinds of questions are *not* the type of approach you want to take.

At this stage of a dialogue, the kinds of questions you *don't* ask are every bit as important as the questions you *do* ask. So let's take a look at what kinds of pitfalls to avoid in asking questions, so that you don't unwittingly turn into a drill sergeant. Here are some common types of questions that should always raise a red flag.

Irrelevant Questions

Asking questions is generally a good thing. Asking questions for the sake of asking questions, however, can be a very bad thing. When you are clearly pressing and groping for things to ask, you send several messages to the other person, none of them good: I am not focused on what you are saying. I am flustered. This subject does not interest me. I am trying to look good rather than engage you.

A good rule of thumb for an appropriate, relevant question is whether it ultimately moves the discussion closer to a resolution. For example, asking someone if they are upset about what happened can give you important data and show respect, but asking if they get angry a lot does not. This means that sometimes the best questions are prepared in advance before you ever enter the discussion. In general, if the right questions are not coming easily and naturally in a conversation, it might be best to pass them by entirely.

The Question That Isn't a Question

Some people—such as difficult bosses or competitive rivals—tend to ask people lots of questions. These kinds of questions generally have one thing in common:

They aren't really questions. They are statements phrased in the form of a question, designed to evoke an uncomfortable response, and they rarely lead to painless conversations. Here are some examples:

- "What were you thinking?"
- "How did you expect to succeed at that?"
- "Who would do a thing like that?"
- "What is the matter with you?"
- "How many people do you think would use that approach?"

People who ask questions like this do not, in fact, want to know what you were thinking, or that 17 other people would use your approach. They are expressing hostility, in a form designed to force the other person to respond. Just be aware that we are all at risk of asking questions like these when we are sufficiently upset with the other person, and, of course, that they do not count as questions in the sense that we mean them here. They will very quickly take you in the opposite direction from a painless discussion and should be avoided at all costs.

Why Ask, "Why?"

Think back to when you were five years old. Your mother was towering over you with the incriminating evidence of your blue crayon in her hand. Pointing to her brand new wallpaper, now elegantly scribbled over with the best of your artistic talents, she leans over and asks, "Why did you do that?"

So what did you say in response? Did you provide her with an intelligent analysis of what led you to decorate the walls? Or a case-by-case breakdown of your decision-making process? Or an engaging discussion about your development as an artist?

The reality is, you probably looked at your shoes and stammered, "I dunno. It was an accident."

Now fast forward to your life at work today. The boss is towering over you, holding a late report in her hand. Pointing to the calendar, she thunders, "Why wasn't this delivered on time?" How do you answer this, as a mature, professional adult? Let me guess. You probably looked at your shoes and muttered, "I dunno. It was an accident."

Finally, let's turn the situation around. Do you ask people why they have done something that makes you unhappy? What kind of response do you expect?

More important, what kind of response do you get? I will bet you lunch that whatever you hear, it is not productive.

With few exceptions, "why" questions are generally not designed to elicit feedback from people. Instead they are primarily designed to assign blame and express frustration. At another level, they may be intended to understand someone's motivation for their actions, but they are usually worded in a way that puts people on the defensive. They usually yield less clarity, not more.

Help Me Understand

Years ago, this phrase was proposed as a well-intentioned way to ask people to explain behavior you disapprove of. Unfortunately, it is now almost universally interpreted as another flavor of the "why" question, and the listener will process it as "Help me understand why you keep messing up." In general, if you want to learn why something happens, the least effective way to do so is to ask someone to help you understand it.

Inquiring Minds Want to Know

Last but not least, remember that there are personal and privacy boundaries that need to inform your thinking every time you ask a question. It may be OK to ask someone if everything is all right or how her job is going, but in a sensitive discussion, it may be inappropriate to ask her what she did over the weekend or how things are going with her boyfriend.

When people choose to open up and share parts of their personal life as part of a dialogue, being understanding and empathetic is very appropriate, but using questions to probe further into sensitive personal territory crosses a boundary, even if the other person willingly responds in the present moment. Use your judgment in following the other person's lead, but in a sensitive workplace discussion, be careful to keep your questions focused on appropriate work issues.

Boiling down all of these questions into a simple guideline, you want to avoid questions that challenge people, disrespect them, or take you further away from what they are thinking and feeling. Or to put this as an even simpler guideline, trust your gut. If you get that tingling feeling in the pit of your stomach that a question is not going to be well received, it is probably the wrong question.

Conversely, the best guide for effective questions is the response of the other person. The things they say—and occasionally, the things you observe them *not* saying—can give you a sense of when questions will engage someone and move the discussion forward. Used properly, good questions represent a simple and yet powerful way to transition into a painless discussion of even the most sensitive issues.

CHAPTER 5

Normalize: It's OK, Really

I am going to share the plot with you of nearly every detective movie ever made. A bad guy does bad things. The police catch him. Once he is in custody, the Bad Cop comes in, furrows his or her brow, and says things like, "We caught you and now we're going to make you talk." The perp responds defiantly. Then the Bad Cop goes away and the Good Cop comes in.

The Good Cop does not accuse the perp of anything. To the contrary, this officer is full of warmth and understanding. This cop says things like, "I can understand how you feel about that," and "You're not the first person to be in this situation." As they build a dialogue, eventually the Good Cop addresses the crime itself by saying something like, "Look, pal, people get upset with their enemies all the time, and sometimes they take it too far. Tell me honestly what happened." The perp then dissolves in tears, confesses the crime, and then the strings cue to signal the end of the movie.

The classic "good cop, bad cop" technique has been put into action by law enforcement professionals for many years. Police officers know that the way to get hardened criminals into dialogue about very bad things is to let them know that they are far from alone in their feelings and actions. Hopefully you don't make a habit of having feedback dialogues with crooks, but if it works for them, think of what it can do for you when you give other people feedback!

As we mentioned in Chapter 2, this process is known as *normalizing* because it takes the other person's feelings and actions and helps them appear normal, for the purposes of opening up dialogue. In this chapter, we are going to examine this process in detail, and see how becoming a "good cop" will change the dynamics of your own interactions.

WHY EVERYONE HATES NORMALIZING—
AND WHY YOU MUST DO IT ANYWAY

Let's be honest with each other: When you aren't used to doing it, normalizing feels about as natural as hanging by your thumbs. It just feels so wrong to be giving any credit to another person for how they describe a situation when you do not agree with him or her. To the uninitiated, it almost seems like you are caving in to the other person or letting him play games with you and get away with it.

These feelings are very natural because they are part of our innate fight or flight reaction. When we feel challenged by someone, our subconscious springs into action to prepare us for battle, just like we did centuries ago when a hungry predator was in our path. It is a physical reaction as well as an emotional one: If we listen carefully to our own bodies in situations like these, we will find our pulse rate quickens, our pupils dilate, and our muscles tense—all steps designed to help us run away or go into battle with an enemy.

Unfortunately, this means that we are biologically programmed to give no credence whatsoever to the other person. Things like recognizing a grain of truth in what the other person is saying, understanding their point of view, or even cutting them slack for an excuse are simply not on the agenda. This is because every fiber of your being is programmed to defend your interests.

Then there is the moral aspect. At this point, some of you are thinking to yourselves, *What? That is ridiculous! When people do bad things, it isn't 'normal.' When people don't do their jobs, it isn't 'normal.' And when people gossip, backstab, and get people in trouble in my office, it isn't 'normal' either. How can I normalize what other people are doing without being a total hypocrite?* It is perhaps this mental and emotional shift that people find the most difficult about normalizing.

So why should you fight against 10,000 years of human history and normalize the other person's position? For three extremely selfish reasons:

1. *It lowers the heat.* Remember how suspects respond when the "bad cop" comes along, or how you reacted when your parents yelled at you.

We all tend to react negatively, with responses that range from withdrawal to defiance. Conversely, we tend to respond well when people understand us. Both of these are innate emotions that you have the power to choose and trigger in other people.

When you are in a sensitive or difficult conversation with another person, you want to take as much of the heat out of the dialogue as possible.

2. *It opens up space for dialogue.* While criticism usually turns a discussion into a one-way monologue, with a receiver who tunes you out, normalizing what other people say makes it safe for them to talk frankly with you about the issue at hand. The longer you can stay in productive dialogue on a difficult subject, the greater a chance you have of resolving it, and normalizing the other person represents one of the most powerful ways of keeping the other person in dialogue.

This is why normalizing is the single most important technique used in crisis intervention. When people call a crisis hotline, they usually feel that they are totally alone with their problem, whether it is grief, loneliness, behavioral issues, or other concerns. By letting callers know that many other people have experienced feelings like theirs, and that they understand what they are going through, good counselors create a zone of safety where it is OK to talk frankly about whatever the caller is going through.

3. *It gives you power.* As for the moral aspect of normalizing people, relax and listen carefully: Normal does not mean OK. It does not mean desirable. Nor does it mean acceptable. Normal has a very specific, dictionary definition that relates to the actual roots of the word: It describes behavior that is close to a *norm*, in other words, that other people share it. And even the worst behaviors have norms that can be acknowledged while still keeping your integrity—and the dialogue—intact.

Let's drill down a little further on this point. Here are some examples of how you can normalize:

- When someone has erupted in a shouting match at work, you can acknowledge that lots of people feel strong emotions and lose their temper. *You are not agreeing that this is a good thing.*

- When someone is making the umpteenth excuse about being late for work, you can accept that it is hard to come in to work when things like this happen. *You are not telling them that it is OK to keep coming in late for work.*
- When someone blames everyone but herself for a problem that is her fault, you can acknowledge how she feels about the other people. *You are not accepting her explanation that things are their fault.*

In each of these cases, you are understanding and accepting how the other person sees the world, period. You are not being dishonest nor are you agreeing with behaviors you cannot accept. All you are doing is showing people that you understand how they see the world as just one step toward negotiating a solution.

When I teach training courses on managing difficult conversations, I give people a role-playing exercise that almost everyone fails. I have one person pretend to have come in late for the fourth time in two weeks and offer every lame excuse in the book for it: The dog was sick, the car broke down, his girlfriend's parents were visiting, he accidentally knocked over the breakfast table, or whatever.

The other person's job is simple. They are to just stand there and acknowledge everything the other person is saying. They do not need to agree, disagree, or solve the problem; they just need to acknowledge and validate each of the other person's excuses: "It must be really frustrating when your dog is sick." "You're right: having your in-laws visit in the middle of the workweek sounds very stressful." "I hate it when I do things like knock over the breakfast table. You must have been really annoyed."

The same thing happens with nearly every pair who role plays this exercise: The person making up these excuses eats up every word of these acknowledgments and could do this all day, while the other person detests every minute of it. In fact, after about the third excuse, they usually turn to me and exclaim, "I can't do this anymore!"

At this point, I explain to everyone that I will normalize people's behavior all day, all night, or even all week if they wish. Why? *Because it gives me power in a difficult discussion.* It completely dissipates the energy that people put into defending themselves, and lets us focus completely on the issue at hand once they are done speaking. If it didn't feel so *wrong* to be validating the other person, we would all be doing it naturally, and in the process, we would all be having much more productive and focused conversations. So now let's look at the mechanics of how to normalize anything someone else says.

HOW TO NORMALIZE FEELINGS IN THREE EASY STEPS

If you are like most people and aren't used to normalizing the feelings of people you disagree with, you will notice two things immediately once you try it. First, it feels funny! This is a very common reaction, because at least at first, your words are not following your gut feelings. So until you get used to it, it feels a little like acting.

Second, and more important, it is hard to find the right words to say. This is also very understandable, once again because your thoughts and emotions keep trying to push your "criticism" buttons instead of your "understanding" buttons. As a result, many people fall back on the dreaded catch phrase "I understand," or a half-hearted repetition of what the other person says when they are first trying to normalize.

The good news is that normalizing statements are normally very procedural and mechanical, and you will get much better over time as you practice using them. In general, they take one of three specific forms:

1. *Acknowledgment:* You recognize the other person's feelings.
2. *Validation:* You accept the other person's feelings as being valid.
3. *Identification:* You identify yourself or others as having experienced the other person's feelings.

You can think of these types of statements much like three octane levels of fuel, because each involves a different level of emotional investment, and each has a progressively stronger impact on the other person. Acknowledgment requires almost no personal emotional investment on your end and has a mild but still positive impact. Validation involves a little more investment and has a greater impact. And identification, when you can use it honestly and authentically, creates the greatest effect of all.

Above all, each of these types of normalizing statements is substantially more effective than our usual responses to people. Here is how they break down:

Acknowledgment

Acknowledgment is, for most people, one of the easiest places to start when you are trying to normalize another person's feelings. At this stage, all you are doing is paraphrasing the other person's feelings *as he or she sees them*, but without implying that you agree or disagree with what is being said. Here are some examples:

> **EMPLOYEE:** I can't finish this project on time!
> **You:** So you are feeling like this project needs more time and resources.

> **COLLEAGUE:** I hate the way Gunther always tries to take charge.
> **You:** I can tell that Gunther is getting under your skin.

> **SUPERVISOR:** People need to start working harder around here.
> **You:** It sounds like you aren't happy with our team's productivity.

What makes acknowledgments like these relatively painless is that they require you to insert none of your own feelings at all into the discussion. You may empathize with the other person, totally disagree with him, or have no respect for what he is saying, and still be implying no dishonesty whatsoever with these responses. You are simply clarifying what you hear in a way that engages him to talk further.

The key to an effective acknowledgment is to paraphrase and not simply repeat the other person's words. Take what this person tells you, and play it back in your own words, so that the listener understands that you heard and processed what he or she is saying. Then leave time and space for the other person to respond and continue moving forward from there.

Validation

If acknowledgment is an entry-level form of normalizing, validation is the graduate course. As its name implies, when you validate someone's feelings, you say things designed to imply that these feelings are *valid*. Here are some examples of how to use validation with the same statements we just examined:

> **EMPLOYEE:** I can't finish this project on time!
> **You:** It is really frustrating to be crunched for time.

Colleague: I hate the way Gunther always tries to take charge.
You: No one likes feeling bossed around.

Supervisor: People need to start working harder around here.
You: I can't blame you for wanting people to be more productive.

Once again, you are generally on solid ground using validation no matter how you feel about the other person's statements, because *feelings are never wrong*. Of course, there are limits: for example, if someone says, "Gosh, I would like to rob a bank," you would probably not respond by saying that lots of banks get robbed every year! But for the most part, the extra emotional investment of validating someone pays off in more productive dialogues, because you are framing your responses from a position of respect.

Identification

This is the post-graduate course in normalizing someone because it unleashes the most powerful weapon for making someone feel accepted—your own experience, expressed as what you have observed in yourself or others. Here is how it might play out with these same three statements from before:

Employee: I can't finish this project on time!
You: I often feel that I can't meet my deadlines either.

Colleague: I hate the way Gunther always tries to take charge.
You: I hate it when someone bosses me around, too.

Supervisor: People need to start working harder around here.
You: You aren't the only person who feels that way.

Note carefully that identification *still* does not imply that you agree with the other person; it only means that you both share common feelings and experiences. This means that you can use it a lot more often than you think:

- You can acknowledge that you have felt deadline pressures even when you feel that you work harder than the other person.

- You can acknowledge that you don't like being pushed around even when you feel that the other person could do a much better job of standing up for herself.
- You can share that other people share someone's view on productivity even when you feel this person is an unrealistic slave driver.

The key here is that going against our natural instincts and identifying with someone puts you at the top of the mountain of credibility. When two people disagree with each other, it almost always involves either or both parties feeling like the other person does not understand them. When you normalize someone, and particularly when you can effectively use identification, you take that chess piece off the table entirely and speak with authority from the voice of someone who knows their side as well as yours.

Are there ever times when you should not identify with someone? Absolutely. When the other person's behavior crosses a serious boundary, you do not want to create the zone of acceptance and respect that identification implies: for example, if someone gets angry and starts throwing things, it may be OK to use acknowledgment ("I can tell you are very upset") but certainly not identification ("I feel like throwing things sometimes too"). Likewise, if someone has embezzled half your company's profits, you may want to let the police do the normalizing. But in general, identification with even bad things can send a very powerful symbol that you have shared the other person's experience and learned from it.

These three normalizing techniques can be employed to suit whatever "octane level" you feel is appropriate to the situation—depending upon the other person's mood and feelings, the gravity of the situation, how hard it is to engage the other person, and above all your gut feelings. In general, the more personally you can engage the other person, the better, within the bounds of propriety and the situation. That said, each of these approaches will help difficult conversations become more productive, particularly when the other person's behavior is uncomfortable to discuss head on.

NORMALIZATION: THE BENEFITS ARE MORE THAN SKIN DEEP

As we mentioned before, normalizing people's feelings is a very mechanical process. Most people can grasp the practicalities of acknowledging, validating, and identifying with people fairly quickly—and then you can apply these techniques with very little thinking required. But when you actually start using these techniques in a difficult dialogue, something truly amazing happens: You start to *feel* differently about the other person.

This, ultimately, is the higher purpose of using normalizing. It is designed to frame the discussion as one where anything can be safely talked about, particularly in adversarial situations. In the process, it creates an unspoken agreement on both sides to talk about difficult situations with professionalism and respect. By using this approach, for as long as the other person wishes to express an opinion, you remove one of the key stumbling blocks to effective dialogue.

The process does not stop with normalizing, of course. Next, we will look at how to discuss issues frankly and completely now that we have laid the groundwork through using a neutral opening, asking good questions, and acknowledging and validating the other person's view of the world. By returning to these safe places as often as needed, you will find that you have a sense of confidence and control in difficult conversations that most people could never imagine.

CHAPTER 6

Discuss the Issue:
Just the Facts

U p to this point, everything we have discussed essentially serves to make the discussion easier on both sides. The techniques we have learned so far have been relatively easy to learn and use, but they aren't enough by themselves. For example, some people have reported going through an entire termination interview with their human resources departments and having no idea that they were being fired! At some point, you must shift gears decisively into a frank discussion of the issue between you and another person.

So guess what? This part is easy too. In fact, it is even easier than the previous steps because it involves three simple steps that make perfect sense in hindsight. They are so easy that I call them the three E's:

- Take the *emotion* out of the issue.
- *Engage* the other person in solving the issue.
- *Empathize* with each and every response.

The catch is that when someone keeps breaking the rules, or isn't pulling their weight, or has annoying personal issues, these steps are all the opposite of what most of us do. We show our emotions, we bark orders instead of engaging the other person, and empathy is the furthest thing from our minds. That is why this is a process rather than just an attitude. You need to learn and practice the steps beforehand. But once you learn this process, it will feel so natural that its effectiveness alone will motivate you to keep using it. Look at these examples:

The Problem	How to Discuss It
Your performance hasn't been up to par lately.	Normally, a typical employee produces about 100 widgets an hour. Your productivity has been about 40 per hour recently. What do you think might be the reasons for this?
Your short temper is getting on everyone's nerves lately.	I sense that you are feeling angry a lot lately, and it has been impacting other people's morale. What do you think might help solve the problem from here?
You are dropping the ball on important customer issues.	Several customers have been sharing concerns about getting follow-up on their issues recently. What is your take on the situation?

Each of these examples show you how you can take what would otherwise be an emotionally-charged discussion, and turn it into a factual problem-solving session—hopefully without triggering the natural defensive responses of the other person—which in turn moves you more quickly toward a productive solution. Now let's break down the mechanics of the process.

STEP 1: TAKE THE EMOTION OUT OF THE ISSUE

Think about the last time your favorite sports team lost a game. How did people describe it? Probably in terms like these:

- "They stunk up the field."
- "They choked."
- "That umpire couldn't see what happened if you bought him binoculars."
- "The players acted like they didn't even care."
- "They played like a bunch of losers."

In reality, they probably did none of these things, at least not in any literal sense. What really happened was probably more practical and technical. They missed an opportunity to score, they were outrun or caught short at a critical moment, or they could not keep up with a competitor who was having a great night.

This distinction is critically important because you cannot do anything about intangible things like "choking," but you *can* do something about the mechanics of giving up a score. This is exactly how I want you to approach your toughest workplace discussions—by laying an issue out on the table, sucking all the emotion out of it first, and then speaking to the nuts and bolts of it.

Up to this point, you have accomplished something extremely valuable. By starting the conversation in a neutral place, asking questions, and normalizing the other person's feelings, you have built a relationship that is conducive to productive dialogue. That is why discussing the issue itself is the fourth step of the process and not the first step. Now you want to keep this momentum going by talking about something that no one can argue with: the facts.

In the process, you will discover one of the great unspoken secrets of human nature, which is that most of us do not process another person's emotions very well. If we call someone a goof-off, she is not likely to respond productively unless she has the patience of Mahatma Gandhi. But if you tell her she is not handling as many cases per day as her peers, and you have already demonstrated that you understand her, you are much more likely to have the issue addressed. Look at these examples and see what we mean:

Feelings	Facts
You are undermining my authority.	When you and I tell employees different things, they feel conflicted.
You aren't pulling your weight.	Your sales are 20 percent less than the company average.
You are loud and annoying.	When you have spirited phone conversations, it distracts people in the surrounding cubicles from their work.
You are mean to people.	You make critical comments to people about their work that make them feel angry and less productive.
You don't have a clue what you are doing.	You missed several steps in our normal procedure for doing this task.

What most people do not realize is that you cannot do anything about the issues in the first column, other than make people defensive or, perhaps once in a great while, scare them into grudging, foot-dragging cooperation. Conversely, the things in the second column are all facts that you can talk about dispassionately and troubleshoot within an atmosphere of mutual respect and problem solving.

When you learn the gentle art of leading into a discussion respectfully and describing issues factually, there is generally no limit on how frank you can be with the other person. I firmly believe in hitting important issues right between the eyes, and a fact-based discussion lets you do exactly that—painlessly.

STEP 2: ENGAGE THE OTHER PERSON IN SOLVING THE ISSUE

Up to this point, questions have been a useful tool for getting and staying in dialogue. At this stage of the conversation, they become critical. Asking someone what they think in a nonthreatening way lies at the core of turning a difficult issue into behavioral change. Here are some examples of good questions for this stage of the discussion:

- "What do you think?"
- "How do you feel we should address this?"
- "If you were in my shoes, what would you do?"
- "Where can we go from here?"
- "What options would make the most sense to you?"

Adding a question to this part of the process as we have done in each of these examples accomplishes two very important objectives: It shows trust in the other person to help resolve an issue, and it gives them an opportunity to take ownership of the solution. Neither of these two things usually happen when you simply tell someone what to do.

The other person's response may or may not be productive at this stage, but either way, you have opened a dialogue that will hopefully lead you both toward an eventual solution, as long as you *keep acknowledging the other person's answers* and *use them as a starting point to explore alternatives*. For example, let's play out one of the scenarios we mentioned earlier and see where it goes:

You: Normally, a typical employee produces about 100 widgets an hour. Your productivity has been about 40 per hour recently. What do you think might be the reasons for that?

Employee: Oh, I don't know. These new machines are so much harder to use than the old ones.

You: Sometimes it's really hard to change something you've done for a long time. Do you think more training might help?

Employee: Well, to be honest, I'm not very comfortable using computers, and this computerized equipment has really been a problem for me.

You: You have a lot of company these days. Perhaps we could explore some alternatives and see where we might go from here.

As we discussed previously in Chapter 4, the type of question that you ask is critical here. Even in contentious situations—*especially* in contentious situations—you should take great pains to make sure that your questions are productive, nonthreatening, and solution-oriented. This means that many of the questions people have been taught to ask in employee situations should frankly go out the window. This is not because they aren't appropriate, but because they simply do not work. For example, let's look at a traditional disciplinary interview question for someone who is excessively tardy:

"Can we expect you to start coming in on time from now on?"

This sounds like a reasonable question to ask someone who is frequently coming in late, at least on paper. But when you break down the mechanics of it, look closer at what you will find:

- It is a confrontational, humiliating question designed to put the other person on the defensive.
- It is a closed question that limits discussion. The employee in question may simply be thoughtless or disorganized, or she may be taking care of her terminally ill mother. This question doesn't facilitate a realistic discussion of the options you both have in each of these cases.
- There is only one answer to this question. If this employee is bound and determined to never come in late again, she will respond "yes." If she is stressed, disengaged, or hates her job, she will also answer

"yes." You will learn nothing from the answer, nor does it correlate particularly well with how the other person will actually behave.

Overall, this question serves just one purpose: to assert your authority and intimidate the other person into compliance. Perhaps you will get the behavior you want in response to this, and perhaps you won't. These discussions are no fun on either side. And either way, we can guarantee you will probably never win the Boss of the Year award asking questions like these.

I want something much better for you in situations like these. I want people to be totally honest with you, I want you to fully understand the context of the situation, and above all, I want you to motivate people to *want* to change. All of this, in turn, will give you your best chance of success. And I want the discussion to be a *painless* process on both sides. So now let's switch gears and try one of the questions we discussed earlier:

"Where can we go from here on this issue?"

Depending on the situation, the results of this question might be very different:

- The person may realize the importance of this without feeling defensive and stop coming in late.
- You may discover that the other person has life issues that make it hard for her to come in on time, such as health issues or caregiving. This information might open up other options such as shift changes, more flexible assignments, or other ideas.
- This person may be honest with you that tardiness has been a lifelong struggle for her, and this discussion may lead to exploring responsibilities that are less time-critical so you can continue to use her talents.

Granted, these examples may not reflect the options you have in your workplace. For example, everyone may have to come in on time in every position, or this person may have the kind of specialized responsibilities where you have no flexibility to offer them. Either way, the principle remains the same: the right kind of open questions, designed to engage someone about a difficult or sensitive issue, are the key to the kind of honest, authentic dialogue that is more likely to lead to the behavioral change you are seeking.

If we are honest with ourselves, most of us would not normally think to engage people when we are having a difficult discussion. We would rather do what humans naturally do, which is to simply tell people what to do and hope they will do it. This is why learning to ask open, nonjudgmental questions will help you stand out from other people, discuss issues much more painlessly on both sides, and above all, get much better results. With practice, you will find that the right questions are one of the most powerful ways to connect with people in your most sensitive discussions.

STEP 3: EMPATHIZE WITH EACH AND EVERY RESPONSE

Remember how we discussed in a previous chapter how important it is to acknowledge and validate the other person's feelings? Well guess what? It is doubly important to do the same thing when you are in the heat of discussing the issue. Empathizing with people each and every time they speak gives you the credibility to negotiate the issue in good faith. Compare these two examples:

Not so good:

> **You:** When you argue with people and call them names, it affects their morale and productivity.
> **Rufus:** But these people never cooperate with me!
> **You:** But you start most of the fights.
> **Rufus:** If these people gave a hoot, I wouldn't fight with them! It's all their fault.

Better:

> **You:** When you argue with people and call them names, it affects their morale and productivity.
> **Rufus:** But these people never cooperate with me!
> **You:** I can tell you are frustrated by how people react to you. I don't like it when people push me off either. Perhaps we can explore some ways to get more cooperation out of them from here.
> **Rufus:** OK, tell me more.

Here you can see in black and white that empathizing has nothing to do with being nice to people and everything to do with achieving your objectives.

In the first case, this discussion could easily go on all day, like a tennis match where you lob each other's agendas back over the net to each other. You would both probably leave this discussion exhausted and upset with each other. But in the second case, you are painlessly moving the discussion toward exactly what you want to talk about: *how Rufus should treat other people*. And you do it by giving Rufus credibility for his feelings, each and every time.

DO EMOTIONS HAVE A PLACE IN THE DIALOGUE?

In general, each step of this approach uses a gentle, nonconfrontational approach to even very tough issues. This begs a larger question: Should you ever show your emotions in a difficult conversation? Or are you forever doomed to sounding like Mr. Spock in the television series *Star Trek*, the half-Vulcan, half-human science officer who solved everything through logic and reason?

The answer is, it depends. In general, you should remember two key principles when you are having a sensitive discussion:

1. Threatening another person triggers natural defensive reactions that generally make it *harder* to reach a successful conclusion.
2. Showing anger almost always makes a permanent change in your relationship with the other person.

That said, there are times when your emotions are, in fact, an important part of the discussion, such as when something has affected you very personally, or when the other person has crossed a serious boundary. (If someone threatened your child, for example, you would have a very hard time holding a neutral, dispassionate discussion—as would most of us!) In these cases, the most productive way to address these situations is to make these emotions part of the facts of the situation. For example:

"I was very upset about what you said about me yesterday and I'd like to talk about it."

There are, in fact, situations that must cross the boundaries of diplomacy, such as when issues of power, control, or safety are involved. For example, police officers often must exert command and control over others to keep a situation safe, and substance abuse counselors may need "tough love" to break through the defenses of an addict who is used to lying and manipulating her way out of situations. Just make sure that you treat these situations as the exceptions that they are, and keep the focus of most discussions on a productive, problem-solving approach based around the facts of the situation.

So now you are in the home stretch of handling very difficult conversations in the workplace. You have started in a safe place, asked questions, and normalized the other person's feelings. And now you have opened up a painless and factual discussion of the issue at hand, using a simple process that drains all of the emotion out of a tough situation and focuses both parties on a solution. Read on and learn how to bring what is now an already painless discussion to an even more painless end.

CHAPTER 7

Incentivize:
It's All About Them

A psychology professor recently told me an interesting story about the early days of his own private practice when he often worked with at-risk youth. As a bright young therapist, fresh from learning the very latest in communication skills, he imagined himself helping these youth examine the choices they were making and hopefully leading them to make some positive changes.

Except that it didn't quite work that way. Adolescents tuned him out. They were about as interested in examining their "choices" as you are about doing your taxes. And the last thing they needed was another surrogate parent figure trying to nudge them toward doing the right thing.

For this therapist, who was a very quick study, the breakthrough came when he started focusing on their own interests. Eventually it became common for him to greet a new client with questions like, "What is it like to be you?" and soon kids were holding forth about things like rap music, friends, TV shows—and honest feelings. He even tried his hand at writing a few stanzas of rap himself, in order to communicate on their level. His ability to help understand and change young people revolved almost completely around learning what pleasures made them tick.

It is exactly the same thing with the people with whom you interact. You can talk all day about what you want, what the rules are, or how much you want them to change their behavior. But if you want to create lasting, self-sustaining change in other people, you must find the incentives that motivate *them* to want what you are looking for.

Once you have taken a dialogue with someone to the point where you have discussed the issue at hand frankly, the next critical step is to explore the incentives to the other person. Very few people ever do this naturally, but when you learn the mechanics of it, the level of influence and credibility you will have with others will increase dramatically.

This chapter will show you how to recognize these incentives and leverage them to help both parties get more of what they want. First, let's look at why incentives are one of the first places you should look in a difficult conversation.

THE LADDER OF INCENTIVE

However nice we may be, we too often look at people as obstacles to overcome or objects to control. You can tell people to do things. If you have authority over them, you can even force them to comply. But unless you can find their incentives—the things they think about and long for—and tap into these incentives, you have little or no chance to influence them. Simply put:

No incentive = No leverage

You might be reading this and thinking to yourself, "Now just a minute! I give people feedback when people are doing things wrong. It's *their* responsibility to do their jobs well. It shouldn't be *my* job to give them incentives to cooperate. Why shouldn't I just tell them to cut the comedy and stop doing bad or stupid things?"

Well, first of all, you are absolutely correct. It is their responsibility to do the right thing. The problem is that deep down inside, they don't really care what you want. This becomes particularly vexing when the other person is doing something really bad. But ironically, the worse the other person's behavior is, the more important it is that you speak to their interests. I could express this visually as a ladder that goes from the bottom to the top of the things that motivate each person. See the illustration at the top of the next page.

At the bottom of the ladder is all the stuff that is least important to them. These would include things like adhering to company policy, following the rules, coloring inside the lines, or avoiding punishment. And if most of us are honest with ourselves, listening to what you have to say probably ranks some-

The Ladder of Incentives

The tippy-top: hopes, dreams, success, money, relationships

The middle: the good of the organization, your wishes

The bottom: following rules and policies, avoiding punishment

where in this range as well. These are things people only do because they have to, and are not themselves highly motivating factors.

In the middle are things that have some interest to them but are not at the top of their list. These might include things like making their boss happy, helping their workplace to succeed, and doing the "right thing." These things might matter to people at some level, but in all likelihood they are not the things that they go to bed every night thinking and hoping about.

Which leads us to the top of the ladder. This is the place where people's thoughts live most of the time, surrounded by the things that are most important to them: their family, their relationships, their finances, and their personal success.

So where do we go when we try to give someone feedback? Ironically, most of us start at the base of the ladder. We focus on those things that are precisely the least important to the other person: our rules, our policies, and the other person's deficiencies. These are the things that we very much care about, and may in fact be areas in which we have the power to force the other person to comply. But in terms of getting them to care or buy in, it is precisely the wrong neighborhood to hang out in. Too often the results of a bottom-of-the-ladder conversation are rolled eyes or sarcasm the moment you are out of earshot.

A few of us climb a little higher to the middle rungs of the ladder and speak to things like serving the greater good or pleasing one's superiors. Are these middle rungs more effective at engaging and motivating people? Perhaps. But I want you to go where almost no one ever goes, straight to the tippy-top of the ladder, to that place that taps into the wants, needs, and desires of the other person.

So why should you find the peak of someone else's interests, especially with people you might not be very happy with? Because it is the shortest path to what *you* want. Compare these exchanges and see if you don't agree:

> *Not so good:* "I want you to stop coming in late. It is against company policy."
> *Better:* "You have great management potential here. If you start coming in on time, it will be one less thing standing in the way of better opportunities for you."

> *Not so good:* "You should stop yelling at your employees all the time."
> *Better:* "With your talents, you deserve to have people on your team cooperate with you and respect you. Let's look at how we might make that happen."

> *Not so good:* "You are probably our least motivated salesperson."
> *Better:* "I think that with some coaching, you could be making a lot more money."

These latter statements are simple, logical, and generally very effective. So why do we rarely if ever say them? First, because the other person's interests are usually the last place we think to look in a difficult conversation. We are so inherently programmed to focus on what people do *wrong* that even the nicest people tend to keep their focus there. Second, we cannot easily speak to another person's incentives without planning and preparation. So let's first examine where human nature usually takes us and then explore some more productive ways to change the script.

DRESSING SOMEONE UP WITHOUT DRESSING THEM DOWN

This is a real-life example of what happens when you speak to another person's interest, and more important, why it is so hard for most people.

Before I teach anyone anything in my workshops, I have everyone break into pairs and try an icebreaker exercise. Here is the scenario:

Good news! Your workplace is going to have a very important visit next week from some senior government officials, together with a cable news crew, to spotlight your company as an example of a great workplace. Your company's president and upper management will be accompanying them on this visit as well.

You have been told that the delegation will make a personal visit to your group, which leads to one small problem: the hideous wrinkled plaid shirt your office mate always wears to work, even when other people are dressing up.

Your job, over the next ten minutes, is to take turns coaching the other person about how they should dress for this visit. Good luck and have fun!

After everyone reads this, I turn everyone loose to start trying to convince their partner to wear something different when the VIPs visit.

At this point, note that I have taught them nothing. I have already shared the concept of using strength-based psychology to deliver painless feedback, and given the class a couple of good examples, but I haven't yet shown them any techniques for doing so. This makes it a perfect first exercise because nearly everyone is smart enough to follow my lead and not criticize or force the other person to change their clothes, and yet it forces them to examine how "nice" people try to motivate another person to change. When they try to do this, most of their responses fall into one of three predictable patterns.

1. *How's the weather?* This is far and away the most common opening that I observe people using when they are trying to have a feedback discussion with someone, both in role play and in real life. They try to build a relationship with the other person by asking them about their job, their kids, or how the Mets did in the ninth inning last night. In other words, they start with off-topic small talk designed to lead in to the subject at hand. Then, uncomfortably, they shift gears and start talking about what the other person is going to wear.

As we discussed in Chapter 3 about neutral openings, this approach is often the worst of both worlds. First, it makes the eventual negative message seem worse, not better. Second, if you are not already in a comfortable rhythm of engaging this person at other times, this kind of small talk seems forced and transparent. In exercises like this, people often report that they know exactly what is coming next and start to stiffen up as a result. Worst of all, they offer you no chance to speak to another person's interest. And yet we often keep trying to soften the blow with small talk because it is one of our most familiar refuges.

2. *Follow my lead.* The next most common approach involves "modeling" the desired behavior to the other person, in hopes he will magically follow along. A person engaged in modeling might say, "Since this is such an important occasion, I am going to be wearing my best suit. What are you planning to wear?" Like the first response, it is designed to make the speaker more comfortable by avoiding the awkwardness of directly challenging the other person's behavior. Instead, you hope that the other person will see the light by osmosis, and that your good behavior will simply rub off on him.

Conversation is an art, and in this case the artist has picked up a brush and skillfully painted him- or herself into a corner. This is because approximately 99 percent of the time we role play this scenario, the other person responds by saying something like, "Gosh, good for you! But I prefer to be comfortable so I am planning to show up in my same old plaid shirt. You like plaid, don't you?" At which point the first person often rolls her eyes, breaks out of role play, looks at me, and says, "Now what?" (And by the way, I'll tell you what in just a moment.)

3. *The higher purpose.* Finally, some people appeal to the good of the organization. They will often acknowledge that the other person likes to be comfortable (a really good thing, by the way), and then tell this person how important this visit is to the company.

The response to this, even in role play, is again quite predictable: The other person digs his heels in and starts defending his right to wear what he wants. In fact it is ironic that this kind of coaching—which is meant to acknowledge the other person more than the other two approaches above—usually ends up with him getting angrier.

This brings me to the real point of this exercise. If you take someone who wears a wrinkled plaid shirt to work every day and write up a list of the top ten things that motivate him, making your company look good probably isn't high on the scale. It isn't on most people's radar so its usefulness as a motivational tool is extremely limited. Unless you happen to hit the jackpot and find yourself with someone who both dresses poorly and swells with organizational pride, you are out of luck.

This is exactly why I want you to aim straight for the tippy-top of the ladder. For example, here is what I might say in a situation like this:

> "I see this as a leadership opportunity for you. You have a chance for our top people to see how well you come across in a very public situation. That's why, even though I respect that you like to be comfortable, I would like to show you how our most trusted and visible people would dress for a delegation like this. What would you think about that?"

What I have done is taken what I want to happen, looked for its single biggest benefit to the other person, and then proceeded to march straight down Broadway with it. No criticism, no beating around the bush, and no trying to force our will on the other person. We are simply taking a big, fat benefit and dangling it in front of him, in the form of the issue at hand.

But what if you know up front that leadership is precisely the last thing this person desires? Suppose he couldn't care less about how he comes across to people in management; he would much rather be comfortable. And let us also suppose that letting him dress that way will embarrass everyone, so you still want to do something about it. Now what do you say? In this case, I would change the script to talk about whatever else it is that most benefits the other person:

- If this person gets along well with everyone and likes his coworkers, we might focus on how he will look in front of everyone else by dressing well.
- If this person is very sensitive to criticism, we might talk about how dressing well might change the way people think about him.
- If this person is militant about dressing casually, we might focus on how rising to occasions like these give him the credibility to be independent the rest of the time because it is a thoughtful choice he controls.

What most people hear when people want them to change is one of two things: the sound of people dancing around the issue or the drumbeat of criticism. What you *want* them to hear are three things: benefits, benefits, and more benefits. So now, let's look at how you find these benefits for the person you are talking to, and make it all about them.

THE TREASURE HUNT: FINDING THE BENEFIT

Hopefully you now understand the power and the importance of speaking to another person's benefit. So where do you find these benefits?

The answer is that they live in the rhythm of your relationship with another person. For some people with whom you have regular contact, you may have a gold mine of verbal cues that give you a sense of his or her priorities. For others, their position, workplace activities, or outside interests may give a clue to what motivates them. And for those with whom you are more distant, an educated guess based on human nature may be the place where you start.

Here are some places where you can start looking for benefits to bring into dialogue with someone:

Likes and Dislikes

Humans are constantly trading information with each other. Like animals who leave a trail of scents behind, people give you verbal cues that help you understand who they are and what they value. Sometimes these are obvious and sometimes they are subtle, but in most cases, they are there if you look for them.

Since sensitive conversations often involve people who express a lot of negativity, it is particularly important to note that another person's benefits often lie on the other side of their complaints. Here are some examples:

What They Say	What May Benefit Them
They complain constantly about other people.	People respecting them or not criticizing them.
They don't feel they make enough money, or have enough responsibility.	Promotional opportunity.
They don't feel enough respect from others.	Leadership and a voice in the organization.
They dislike their job.	New responsibilities or a change of scenery.
They don't get taken seriously.	Communication skills that give them more power and authority.

Does this mean that you start dangling personal self-improvement benefits in front of people who act like disgruntled employees? In my view, yes. In those cases where I have seen such employees actually turn around their performance, which is what most of us really want to accomplish, the turning point often revolves around a growth opportunity for the other person, along with faith in this person's ability to reach it.

Hopes and Aspirations

Beyond likes and dislikes, most people have things they wish for. They could be as simple as having more time off, or as ambitious as wanting to occupy the CEO's chair some day.

Often one of the biggest determinants in the path of a person's life is what they say about themselves. For example, bestselling novelist Tom Clancy reportedly told people about his literary intentions when he was still a Maryland insurance agent in his 40s, and legendary automotive giant Lee Iacocca writes of his management ambitions already becoming apparent to him as a young engineer.

When people drop hints about the direction they want their life to take, you are getting feedback that is even more valuable than a person's likes or dislikes because it points to something much more important: motivation. People who have goals for themselves beyond simply punching in every day are handing you a gift that you can often use to leverage what will benefit them the most in a situation. For example:

"I know you want to get ahead here, and I can show you how to handle conflicts like these in ways that will gain you more respect."

"You often talk about wanting to move into operations. Learning to do this job well has a lot of competencies that will help you get there."

"You mentioned that you have fantasies of chucking it all and opening a gift shop. The skills you practice in this situation will help you deal with your own employees better."

At the same time, there is an important caution in speaking to another person's hopes and dreams: You are often treading on very personal territory. This means that you need to work harder than ever to keep what you say completely benefit-focused. When you slip into linking these goals to criticisms like, "How can you expect to advance when you act like this?"—or worse, cynically use them to try and manipulate people—you risk violating a very personal bond of trust and closing the door to effective communication in the future. Use people's aspirations to help them succeed, and more important, to help you focus on creating positive, benefit-driven messages.

Things They Value

Each and every one of us has a personal value system. Moreover, these values vary from person to person. Outgoing Amy may crave the spotlight, while quiet and hardworking Pramesh may value a workplace that is free of conflict. In a very real sense, each person carries around his or her own "corporate culture," and we each ultimately become walking advertisements for the things we value.

Here, you can use an approach that I call the playback technique to link these values with the subject at hand. Its name comes from taking what the other person says, thinks, or feels and making these ideas part of your response. A playback statement normally takes a form such as one of the following:

"Because you _____, I am going to recommend _____."
"Since you _____, have your considered _____?"
"I respect your feelings about _____. What would you think about _____?"

This is one of the easier ways to construct a benefit statement because you are starting with things you either know about people or are perhaps learning in the course of the dialogue. Then you are taking these pieces of knowledge, adding a benefit, gift wrapping all of this in your own words, and handing them back to the other person. Some real-world examples of this technique might include the following:

"You hate it when people yell at you. Would you like to learn how to respond to people so they never do that?"
"I know you value harmony among your staff. Let's look together at some ways we might handle making a tough decision like this."
"You are a very performance-oriented manager who wishes people would buckle down and work harder. I have some ideas about how you might accomplish that."

Playback statements are very powerful because they use a fundamental technique that is often practiced in psychotherapy: paraphrasing the other person's thoughts and feelings to open dialogue and stimulate solutions. Its power lies in the fact that it is so infrequently practiced. While most of us justifiably feel that we are nice people, listen carefully to the conversations around you some day and see how rarely people ever actually paraphrase and acknowledge what the other person says.

As with the other kinds of benefits, using the playback approach puts a substantial burden of honesty and authenticity on you. If the things you acknowledge and the things you suggest aren't congruent with each other, you are putting the other person's trust at risk. For example, if you say something like, "I realize you feel people are overworked here, but here is why I'd like you to work even harder," you are losing your credibility to influence this person—often permanently. In this sense, the playback technique can ironically be your best friend because using it effectively forces you to start thinking like the other person before you ever open your mouth.

All of these techniques for finding benefits have one thing in common: Each one requires you to thoughtfully focus on the other person before you start talking about how they need to them to sell more, complain less, or change their clothes more frequently. Done well, they help the other person feel that you really know how they think, which in turn will lead to substantially more cooperation. Better yet, you will find that they change the way you look at people over time and will help you adopt a benefit-driven stance that will fundamentally change the amount of influence you have with others.

NEGATIVE BENEFITS: THE CARROT VERSUS THE TWO-BY-FOUR

This leads us to an open question that is usually one of the first things to come up in a workshop on this topic: Does avoiding negative consequences ever serve as a benefit to the other person?

Many of us remember being punished by our parents and being told, "This is for your own good." We generally didn't agree with this view at the time, but now that most of us are old enough to be parents ourselves, we find that "tough love" sometimes seems like a very seductive way to try and get people to change, particularly when these people are behaving in ways that really push our buttons.

Suppose that someone is constantly late with their projects, so much so that it is threatening their job. What would motivate them to change this? In fact, what would be the most important incentive of all for them? When I throw this question out to students in my workshops, the immediate, knee-jerk answer is always the same: "So they don't lose their job."

So let me ask you a question: Think back to your childhood. Think about your hopes, your dreams, and the things you wanted the most in life. Did they revolve around not getting in trouble with your parents? The reality is, most children face clear sanctions for not behaving the way they should. But as any parent will tell you, the threat of punishment does not in and of itself guarantee perfect children.

In fact, let's take this a step further. Remember what we said at the beginning of this chapter, about how my colleague treats children as a therapist? Good family therapists generally learn what motivates a child, often asking questions that have never been asked by parents or others, and help these children use their behavior to reach the goals *they* have for *themselves*. Instead of using coercion that produces short-term results at best, they tap into a groundswell of motivation that produces real, lasting change.

So now let's circle back to the person who is constantly missing deadlines at work. When you use "keeping your job" as an incentive for this person, you are behaving more like the exasperated parent than the therapist. And unfortunately, you are probably doomed to the same results that these parents get. This is what I call "getting out the two-by-four," or trying to motivate someone through fear.

In cases like these, you need to think hard about what other benefits there are for the other person changing their behavior—in other words, WIIFM (what's in it for me). And don't settle for just any benefit, aim for whatever is at the tippy-top for this person. Our human nature almost always leads to focus on another person's flaws and think exclusively in terms of corrective action without ever realizing that having faith in people in difficult situations can be transformational moments.

Are there times when motivating through fear is necessary? Sure there are. When the gravity of the situation is so urgent that the other person must act at once, then you may need to focus on the consequences. When a building is burning down, you aren't going to start engaging people in a rational discussion about the benefits of leaving. To the contrary, you are going to run around yelling, "Fire!" Likewise, when someone's behavior in the workplace crosses important boundaries, you may need to focus on the consequences.

There may also be situations where there are simply no other incentives for the other person. They may not care about anything other than keeping their job, not losing a bonus, or keeping out of trouble with the boss. My point is that these situations are far fewer than you think. So let's examine what happens when your best efforts at finding an incentive are not working and find out what to do next.

THE "UH-OH" MOMENT

So far, we have described a relatively straightforward process of finding the thing that is most of interest to the other person, and then speaking to that interest. But what happens when you guess wrong?

I call this the "uh-oh" moment because it is one of the most common places where people get stuck in a difficult discussion. It often happens when we do a poor job of reading the other person's interests and hope this person takes the hint anyway. For example, we might say something like, "Wouldn't you like to do things this way?" and the answer is no they wouldn't. But this can also happen when we make our best efforts to understand another person, stroke them with things like future potential or rewards, and it becomes clear they have no interest in what we are offering.

This becomes an "uh-oh" moment because we sit there and wonder what to tell the other person next—and as we covered in Chapter 4, I don't want you to *tell* them anything. I want you to *ask* them what kinds of things would benefit them. When you ask people about their favorite subject—themselves—most are never at a loss for words, and all you need to do is sit back, relax, and provide the airtime for them. Here are some examples:

Situation: The other person treats other people shabbily.
No-Benefit Statement: "You should stop being so difficult with others."
Benefit Question: "How would you like people to react to you in the future?"

Situation: The other person acts like an unmotivated slug at work.
No-Benefit Statement: "You really need to pick up the pace and act like you give a hoot."
Benefit Question: "What kinds of things would make you happier at work?"

Situation: The other person is a hyper-perfectionist whose nitpicking drives everyone nuts, and of course she feels she is right.

No-Benefit Statement: "You are ten times as fussy as everyone else here."

Benefit Question: "How do you think we could get everyone to feel good about meeting a common standard of quality?"

Good benefit questions have three things in common:

1. *They are open questions.* You want to ask questions that ultimately teach you something new about the other person and their motivations. In the examples above, you would not want to ask questions like, "Do you think we should do X?" or "Do you like Y?" These are closed questions that have yes or no answers, and such questions carry too much risk of whizzing right past what the other person thinks and feels. Open questions, which require a thoughtful response rather than a simple "yes" or "no," create space for the other person to share how they honestly feel with you.

2. *They are about the other person.* When you are asking a benefit question, be aware that it is all too easy to slip up and make these questions about *your* benefits. For example, asking, "What would help you improve your performance?" is about *you*, not them. These questions should ideally revolve around their own goals for themselves, whether it helps your organization in the short term or not. In this situation, broader questions like, "What would make you more happy here?" or "What would you do if you ran this place?" are much more likely to tease out an honest and heartfelt answer.

3. *They advocate for the other person.* It often feels funny to speak to someone's interests, particularly when you disagree with her. But by wording your questions in terms of wanting to help this person, you create a social bond that dramatically influences the remainder of the discussion, and makes it much more likely that she will take the benefit you are looking for and drop it in your hand.

One technique that is often used in psychotherapy to help people clarify goals, and that can also be very powerful in helping people set workplace goals, is known as the *miracle question.* It goes something like this:

"If a miracle happened overnight, and this workplace was exactly the way you wanted it to be, what would it look like? What kinds of things would be different?"

What you hear in response is likely to be giftwrapped with the other person's most important goals in the workplace, or even in their personal life. It must be used cautiously and with the right people, namely those who are willing to think creatively and be frank with you. So if you get a response like, "I have no idea" or "If a miracle happened, we wouldn't have to come in here," take the hint and move on. But for those who are willing to put on their thinking caps, questions like these can give you powerful insights that you might never hear in the normal course of the workday.

All of these questions help the other person identify their hopes and dreams in the workplace, but a more subtle benefit is that asking them changes you as much as it changes them. By probing about another person's real feelings and interests, you start to see them holistically as human beings, not just as problems to overcome. This perspective, in turn, will change the things you feel and say to the other person, which can ultimately fuel a different kind of working relationship as well as a more painless dialogue.

Throughout this chapter, we have described a process that goes against most of our natures: seeking and describing benefits for people with whom we are not very happy. Doing it in real life feels funny to nearly everyone at first. Some might even take it a step further and describe it as "sucking up" to someone instead of confronting their problems. For the vast majority of us, there is a little voice in our heads that tells us we should not be looking for benefits, but for a battle to be won.

Here is my perspective, looking back on over a quarter century of management and coaching experience. You need to start ignoring that little voice in your head. It doesn't help you most of the time. It is just plain wrong far too often. And increasingly, it has the entire field of modern psychology lined up against it.

I personally believe that one of the most underutilized discoveries in human communication skills is how the simple phrase "you catch more flies with honey than vinegar" applies to even our most difficult situations. Philosophers hinted at it thousands of years ago, Dale Carnegie wrote books about it over 70 years ago, and now in the 21st century we are finally learning the mechanics of putting it to work in real situations. Always seek the benefits for the person you are talking to and you will find that these benefits come back to you many times over.

Disengage from the Discussion: Making a Good Last Impression

I n the Bible, there is a passage that reads, "The last shall be first, and the first last."[1] They weren't talking about communications skills here. But they are making a point that applies very well to the way you manage a difficult conversation. Most of us should, in fact, take one of the first things we often do in sensitive discussions and make it the very last thing we do—namely, talk about something other than the subject at hand. This chapter will explore how to disengage gracefully from a challenging conversation by shifting back into the rhythm of your normal working relationship.

WHY DISENGAGING FROM THE DISCUSSION IS IMPORTANT

When you wrap up a difficult conversation—especially when you have worked so hard to bring it to a successful conclusion—there are three important reasons to change the subject, each of which touches on the way people process their interactions with each other.

- *People remember the last thing you say.* An interesting quirk of our perception is that we tend to remember things based on how they end. When you get into a knock-down, drag-out fight with someone, but you both end up smiling and shaking hands at the end, that gets burned into our minds as a "good" encounter. Similarly, when you have a perfectly lovely time all day with someone, but end the visit with cross words, that becomes a "bad" encounter. Shifting your focus away from a tough discussion and toward your normal relationship makes the encounter "good" in the other person's mind.

• *People are looking for validation that things are OK.* No matter how strong we are emotionally, none of us likes to be corrected or criticized. This is why, at the end of a difficult conversation, people look for cues about how you still feel about them. By ending on a positive note and moving away from conflict, you reassure the other person that things are still fine between the two of you and that it is OK to move forward from here.

• *Your closing frames the future working relationship.* In addition to wondering if things are OK, people also wonder what their working relationship will be like with you from here. The right kind of closing helps you reconfirm this relationship in a positive and constructive light, which in turn helps your future interactions go more smoothly.

For these reasons, you should always close a difficult conversation by doing what many people would have rather done in the first place: change the subject! Whether you are talking about work, colleagues, or how the team did last night, a positive shift into neutral territory creates goodwill and a productive relationship for the future.

CLOSINGS THAT WORK WELL

There is no single most appropriate way to disengage from an important discussion. Normally your gut feelings are a fairly reasonable guide, where the overall goal is to move away and move on from the issues you discussed. Given this, here are three of the most common ways to disengage successfully.

1. *Discussing Normal Work Issues.* Asking people how their work is going, talking about areas that interest them, or discussing current workplace issues are all very common ways to disengage from the discussion. So long as the interaction is natural, nonthreatening (i.e., not framed as an interrogation), and does not venture into sensitive personal territory,

these are among the more common and appropriate ways to shift out of a difficult conversation.

2. *Sharing Common Interests.* If you are both sports fans, antique collectors, or share another interest in common—and you were both in the rhythm of talking about it before the critical conversation—discussing your existing shared interests is an easy and natural way to exit the discussion.

3. *Looking to the Future.* When it is appropriate, one of the more powerful ways to shift out of an important dialogue is to discuss areas where the participant is valued, respected, and needed in the future. The value of these kinds of closings is that they point to a positive future role in the working relationship while shifting comfortably back into business as usual. Here are some examples:

- "Say, John, would you like to join us at the next planning meeting?"
- "We have a new project starting up soon that I think you might enjoy. Would you like to touch base about it sometime this week?"
- "By the way, we have a new employee who could really use your advice on how this department does things. Would you be interested in spending a little time with her?"

Any of these types of approaches, delivered sincerely, can work very well depending on the state of your relationship with the other person. They are just three of a wide range of responses that close the discussion by moving into safer territory while affirming this relationship for the future. Now let's look at some areas where well-meaning people might stumble in trying to close a difficult conversation.

CLOSINGS TO AVOID

While your gut feelings are normally a fairly reliable indicator of what to say to someone at the close of a conversation, even the best people can stumble if they are not prepared for what to say at the end, particularly if they are scrambling to find a note to end on without thinking things through. The following are some of the ways that good people can inadvertently leave bad impressions when wrapping things up.

> *Offering Gratuitous Praise.* It is human nature when you have just had a very tough discussion with someone to try to say something nice about him or her. It sounds rational and logical, but ironically it is probably one of the last things you should do. Why? Because we are all highly sensitive to any kind of incongruity in others, and we can usually tell when praise is forced and contrived. Unless you are highly talented and sincere, you run the risk of coming across as phony as a three-dollar bill, which in turn can undermine much of the good work you have done to this point.

Now bear in mind that praise is normally a really great thing. I highly recommend using it liberally with people around you. But don't do it right after a difficult conversation unless you truly know what you are doing. Insincere compliments not only risk missing the mark, but also can make you appear uncomfortable and desperate to "smooth things over." Worse, they can undermine your credibility when you compliment this person in the future.

To me, true praise lies in the respect you show people in the course of your normal working relationship with them. When you ask them about their work, share your own feelings, or look to the future, you are implicitly praising and validating them in a way that feels natural on both sides.

I will grant one small exception to this rule: Do you normally say nice things about this person to his or her face? If the answer is yes, then a similar level of praise may be appropriate, particularly if it links back to something you have said before. For example:

> "You know how much I like working with you, so I'm glad we could resolve this situation to everyone's benefit."

The key words here are *you know*: You aren't concocting something nice to say, but rather are linking to a relationship that already exists. Strive for honesty and authenticity and the rest will follow naturally.

> *Setting Expectations.* We have talked about getting back into the rhythm of the workday, but there is one small exception. The tail end of a difficult

conversation is generally not the right place to add to another person's burdens. So tread carefully if you are planning to make more work for someone, and above all, don't mistake this as a means of disengaging from the conversation.

We spoke above about "looking to the future," including some examples of future meetings or projects, but these are examples of things designed to benefit or respect the other person. There is a big difference between talking about an exciting new project and asking someone to stay late and make 500 copies for you, particularly when you have just discussed problems with her work performance.

In general, the rule of thumb is that a good closing should leave the other person feeling good and frame the relationship between the two of you in a more positive direction moving forward. So if at all possible, keep work demands in their proper time and place, and if possible, keep them far away from the closing of a difficult discussion.

Being Inappropriately Personal. I am not talking here about making improper advances toward someone or prying into the listener's personal life, both of which are clearly inappropriate behaviors that go beyond the scope of communications skills. Rather, I am talking about the natural and very common tendency to respond to an emotional experience by talking about yourself, and in the process, disclosing too much to other people.

When you bring a challenging conversation to a successful conclusion, there is often a rush of emotion similar to what happens when you emerge from any tense situation. In the process, some people try to dissipate these feelings by sharing life experiences with the other person. To some extent this is OK within proper workplace boundaries. For example, when you have just successfully coached someone about dealing with their coworkers, it may be appropriate to make a passing comment about dealing with your kids, but it is probably less appropriate to launch into a long monologue about your family relationships.

The key here is that your goal is to re-establish your normal working relationship at the end of an important dialogue. This means that if you are buddies with someone, you should act like a buddy, but if you are this person's supervisor you should act like a supervisor—a warm, caring, and positive supervisor perhaps, but a supervisor nonetheless. A good rule of thumb is that the relationship you had with someone last week, or will have next week, is a good guide for how you want to act as you close the transaction.

THE BEST CLOSING OF ALL

The best way of all to close a discussion with someone, particularly a difficult one, is to say whatever your gut tells you. You have a unique rhythm and context to your working relationship with each person, and this context will in large part determine the best thing to say.

Your working relationship is determined by several factors including the other person's personality, your relative positions within the organization, and above all the outcome of the discussion. You would not ask someone how their garden is doing after you have just demoted them, nor would you get into an animated discussion with someone who is shy and easily intimidated. However, you certainly could discuss future projects with the demoted person to tacitly let them know that life goes on, or quietly engage the shy person about how things are going for them. Your response will be uniquely patterned to a matrix of factors that no one understands better than you.

This brings us to the closing point of ending a discussion, and of the CANDID approach in general: You greatly increase your odds of success when you prepare, rehearse, and write down what you will say at each stage of the process. While no one can anticipate every person's reaction in every situation, being prepared helps you think through these situations ahead of time and gives you confidence. And that, ultimately, is the goal of this entire process: to help you move confidently and painlessly into any situation with any person and bring it to a successful conclusion.

NOTE

1. *The Holy Bible*, English Standard Version, Matthew 20:16.

Section III

The Advanced Course

CHAPTER 9

Reframing: Making Difficult Messages Painless

D id you know that soldiers do not actually shoot at anyone? This is because in the military, they often refer to the process of firing at enemy soldiers as "servicing the target."

What you are seeing here is an example of *reframing*, where something is worded in ways that are less harsh or emotional. Sometimes it can be very beneficial, such as the case where degrading terms like "mentally retarded" are replaced with more accurate ones such as "learning disabled." Other times it can be disingenuous, such as calling a tiny cramped apartment "cozy" in an advertisement. Either way, reframing represents the gentle art of using words to make people feel better.

When you are having a difficult conversation at work, reframing is everyone's friend. Here is why: Suppose that you tell someone that they are slow, or mean, or rude, or incompetent. Or you challenge them about a situation that upset you. Are they likely to agree with you? More important, are they likely to change their behavior? And if other people speak to each other in these terms, are they likely to get along productively?

Reframing is a powerful technique that changes the framework of what you say in ways that change our perceptions. It involves replacing harmful and judgmental observations with neutral and factual ones, which in turn create a basis for productive dialogue. And it is particularly effective when you are dealing with people who, shall we say, feel like a target being serviced.

With reframing, a slow person becomes a methodical one; a fussy person becomes someone with high standards; an incompetent person becomes someone who needs more coaching or a better fit; and an upsetting situation becomes a problem to troubleshoot. It doesn't involve sugarcoating or avoiding legitimate concerns, but rather finding ways to make those concerns safe to talk about. When we change people's perceptions, it is one of the most powerful ways to change our relationships with them. This chapter explores the mechanics of reframing and how you can use it as a key component of making conversations painless at work.

WHY WE DON'T REFRAME—AND WHY WE SHOULD

In an ideal world, we would all describe each other in the most charitable terms possible and live happily ever after. So why do so many of us seem to do exactly the opposite? The answer is simply that our reasons tie in with our human nature, and at a deeper level, our survival instincts.

We tend to magnify our differences. Animals often reject other members of their species that are different. Why is this? Because less-than-perfect specimens can affect an animal colony's ability to hunt food or dodge predators.

Moving forward to the human race, you often see the same kind of dynamic at work. We reject people who are "different," even though no one is hunting us or stopping us from buying Cheerios at the store. Even people who would never consider themselves prejudiced often find themselves rejecting people who are louder, quieter, friendlier, grumpier, or dressed differently from themselves. At one level this can lead to gossip, at another level it can impact your working relationships, and at a darker level it can lead to the kinds of discrimination that we as a society are trying to move past.

We use criticism as a bonding tool. The term clique is defined as a group "held together by common interests, views, or purposes," and forming cliques is part of our nature. While the term may conjure up images of snotty teenagers in a high school cafeteria, in reality any group of people that sees the world the same way—managers, sports fans, quilters, or computer programmers—can form a clique. They can be as small as two or three friends or as large as a corporate culture.

There are two essential ingredients to a clique: a sense of who you are, and a sense of who you are *not*. This is why there is often a strong incentive to gossip about people who aren't like "us," and why this kind of criticism often bonds people closer together. This is a powerful reason why we often don't reframe people or situations because making them look as *bad* as possible becomes part of how we ingratiate ourselves to others.

Many disagreements are in fact personality differences. Think carefully about the people with whom you get along the least well. If you scratch the surface of these relationships, I will wager that you and these people have basic personality differences between you.

Personality defines the way we fundamentally see the world, and according to psychologists, our own personalities are formed in early childhood and tend to vary little throughout our lives. These basic beliefs are generally neither "right" or "wrong," but they strongly influence how we see others. For example, one person may value following the rules while another may feel that making people happy is more important. As a result, the first person may see the other as wishy-washy, while the second sees the other as rigid and hidebound. The irony is that they are both neither completely right nor completely wrong!

When I work with groups dealing with workplace relationships, I have a lot of fun with personality types because they are at the root of so much conflict. I will break people up into corners of the room based on whether they are "feelers," "thinkers," "solid citizens," or "free spirits," and then start firing questions off at everyone like, "How many people hate being told what to do?" or "Who wishes people would shut up and get down to business?" As people see how everyone in one corner raises his hand to one question, and everyone in another corner raises her hand to another, they have an "a-ha!" moment that these people are not wrong—they are just different.

This "a-ha!" moment is the place where reframing lives, and this is why it can dramatically change your working relationships. It uses the power of language to build understanding, change perceptions, and dissolve prejudices. In the process, you not only promote more harmony, but you also set yourself apart as a leader and a diplomat. It's not a bad return on the investment of changing just a few words! Let's look at how the process works.

REFRAMING COMMON ASSUMPTIONS ABOUT PEOPLE

There are three basic ways to approach the process of describing other people in the workplace in a more objective light.

1. *Describe people as they see themselves.* Try this experiment sometime. Listen to people criticize someone, and then go up to the person criticized and ask her how she would describe herself. My guess is that her answer will be very different from that of the critics. And more important, there is probably more than a grain of truth in it!

Of course, some people have a distorted view of their own importance or competencies. But more often than not, most people see the same traits in themselves that other people do; they just frame them differently. By using this frame of reference yourself, you start using a more positive, conflict-free way to characterize people. Here are some examples:

What Others Say	What the Person Herself Says
He is ruthless and demanding.	I am results-oriented.
She is spineless and wishy-washy.	I am accessible and open-minded.
He is scatterbrained and never makes up his mind.	I look at all the possibilities.
She is secretive and tight-lipped.	I think things through before I speak.
He is thin-skinned.	I am sensitive and open with my feelings.

In each of these cases, both sets of statements are probably accurate, depending upon how you interpret them. The descriptions in the second column essentially mirror the ones in the first, but now you are looking at their redeeming qualities as well. By using the phrases in the second column, you are not only describing people charitably but accurately, in both a positive and a negative sense. For example, everyone would agree that you can be *too* sensitive or results-oriented. In the process, however, you are taking much of the heat out of your actual words.

2. *Reduce negative opinions to facts.* Suppose that someone has a trait that is unquestionably negative. We can all agree, for example, that there are no good sides to dressing inappropriately or not working as hard as others. Here you can reframe the discussion from an emotional one to a factual one, as we described in detail in Chapter 6. Here are some examples of reframing people using this technique:

Emotional Description	Factual Description
She is completely out of touch.	She has a management style that was popular 20 years ago.
He is a goof-off.	He takes longer breaks and lunch hours than most people here.
If you lined up people like her from end to end, they would never reach a conclusion.	She does not like to make decisions quickly.
He is not a team player.	He has very specific ideas about what his job responsibilities are.
She can't ever close the deal.	She converts fewer than 40 percent of her leads into purchase orders.

The importance of this kind of reframing is that while the phrases in the first column are purely insults, the phrases in the second column describe problems that can be addressed and solved. You cannot effectively tell someone to be less of a "goof-off." First, it makes the other person resentful and defensive, and second, the term itself is too vague to take action on. You can, however, tell someone to limit their breaks to 15 minutes and come back from lunch at 1 p.m. In the process, you are turning the problem from an emotional one to a behavioral one, and framing it in a way that lets everyone solve it with dignity.

3. *Find the nobler intentions.* This, more than anything, is how psychotherapists use reframing when treating families. For example, a family will often come in hoping to "fix" an unruly teenager, and when the therapist digs deeper, she finds that the teen is constantly being criticized and

disrespected. By reframing their goals from "making our kid behave" to "helping launch Johnny toward a successful adulthood," everyone learns to communicate in a different way.

The same dynamic is constantly in play at your workplace. For example, someone may feel that she is helping create better quality, while others feel she is adding useless busywork. She feels they are opposed to doing the job right, and they feel they are defending their level of productivity. And when everyone speaks to their own agenda, as most of us do, the result is far too many meetings where people's neck veins are bulging out.

Let me teach you how to do a little family therapy in situations like this. First, think through how the other person sees the situation. Find the noblest possible motive for these views. *Then speak to these noble motives when you talk to the other person or about the other person.* Here are some examples:

Not so good: "You are adding a lot of useless paperwork to the process just so you can say we are "six-sigma" or whatever."
Better: "You clearly want to take our quality to the next level. I would like to work with you to try to find the best mix of quality, productivity, and profitability."

Not so good: "Velma is always getting on everyone's case to be quiet."
Better: "Velma puts a lot of value on having a civilized workplace."

Not so good: "You never socialize with anyone around here."
Better: "You respect everyone's privacy and do a good job."

There are two important outcomes to this kind of reframing. First, when you speak to another person's better motives, you create a level of trust and respect that makes any conversation more productive. Second, you often trigger what psychologists call the "Bellac effect," where people behave in ways for which they are recognized. For example, a curmudgeon who is lauded for his concern for the company may, over time, start showing more concern for the people in it as well.

In what is often a very criticism-oriented world, we often lose sight of what happens when we see the good in other people and share it. When you look objectively at the people who frustrate everyone, think of how rarely if ever these people experience praise and support. More important, think about what might happen if they started getting more of it. It is here where reframing has perhaps its most powerful impact.

With each of these approaches, it is important to understand the difference between reframing and sugarcoating the way another person is. In the first case, you describe someone in terms that *most accurately reflect a neutral, objective view of him or her.* In the second case, you are creating an artificially positive view of someone that may or may not correspond to the facts. Compare the difference in this example:

> Original statement: "Dexter is a mean, abrasive son-of-a-gun."
> Reframing: "Dexter vigorously defends his position and is very frank about it."
> Sugarcoating: "Dexter has a spirited style of leadership."

The difference is that most people who agree with statement one would also agree with statement two, but none of them would probably agree with statement three. This underscores the true purpose of reframing: While sugarcoating tends to make apologies for people, reframing casts them in a factual, procedural light that helps others understand their behavior better. In this case the reframed definition of Dexter also shines light onto the path of how to deal with him better, for example, by encouraging people to find nonconfrontational ways to address Dexter's views.

In this sense, reframing serves a practical purpose as well as a healing one. Describing people in more palatable terms is not only more charitable, but also more productive. When it is done properly it gives you more of what *you* want, by framing issues in ways that people can understand and manage. More important, you start building the kind of goodwill that not only improves your relationships with other people, but also can help change the culture of your workplace over time.

HOW TO REFRAME SPECIFIC SITUATIONS

Sometimes issues in the workplace go beyond individual people. For example, a company's management may make an unpopular decision, or the marketplace does not agree with a new product direction. In these cases as well, reframing can turn a very polarizing discussion into a more rational one that is focused on solutions.

Say, for example, that your workplace has recently decided to ban smoking for the sake of everyone's health. Depending on how you feel about smoking—and how you feel about the company—there are several different ways you could describe this situation:

- "The company is trying to look out for everyone's health."
- "They are acting like Big Brother and intruding into our personal lives."
- "Management is paying attention to trends in society."
- "They are trying to save every last nickel on health care costs."
- "This organization realizes that a healthy workforce is a productive one."

Some of these statements defend the company's position; others are critical of it. So my guess is that you will agree with some of them and be frustrated by others, depending upon how you see the world. My position is that you can use reframing in situations like these to address *everyone*, in a way that once again turns an emotional discussion into a factual one. For example:

> "The company is making a change that is going to benefit both its costs for health care and the well-being of its employees, at a cost of requiring people to make sacrifices in their personal choices to smoke."

Now you have a statement that everyone can agree with, phrased in a way that will open rather than limit dialogue. The key here is that the goal of reframing is not to defend a position; it is to describe reality in a factual and nonthreatening way so that people can talk about it. Instead of simply moving an agenda forward, you are opening the door to solutions.

At a broader level, reframing situations well is part of what makes leaders who they are: people who can discuss difficult situations in ways that are frank, honest, and yet productive at the same time. Good politicians are often masters at this skill, and the very best of them often rise above partisan "spin" to inspire all of us. In much the same way, seeking ways to rise above gossip and create inclusiveness through reframing in your own workplace is an important step on your personal path toward leadership.

GETTING PEOPLE ON BOARD WITH REFRAMING

Let's say that you are now convinced about the benefits of reframing. How do you get other people to start using it? By doing a little reframing, of course.

First of all, by simply changing your own pattern of speech and using reframing yourself, the grace and civility with which you discuss things will rub off on other people. Painless conversations become addictive once people see how effectively they work and how powerful they are. Modeling this behavior, in and of itself, is an important way to get people to start reframing themselves.

Now let's move into more sensitive territory: What happens when you are in the middle of a four-star snipe fest, and you would like to get people to start talking more productively? First, I will tell you how *not* to do it. Do not urge people to stop being petty or critical because when you do that, you are not only challenging them, but you are also not modeling the behavior that reframing itself was designed around—presenting things in a factual and nonthreatening light.

Instead, seek what most benefits the other people in the discussion, and start using reframing to pose gentle questions that get the discussion on track. For example:

> "Given that the boss acts this way, what could we productively try to change?"
> "What could we say to this person that might motivate her to cooperate?"
> "How do you feel we could best accomplish what we want out of this situation?"

When you start being a voice for constructive dialogue by reframing and asking productive questions, you accomplish two important things. First, you lower the hostility level in a discussion, and second, you demonstrate to people how much more *they* could accomplish by reframing the things *they* want. Will everyone rise to the occasion and start talking the way you do? No, not always. But if you keep serving as a model for positive, blame-free communications, you will probably find that one person really can make a difference.

This brings home perhaps the most important point of all about reframing. It serves as a more painless way to talk to people, and talk about them. It puts situations in a light where everyone can have a voice and discuss them. But above all, it can serve as a force to bring people together around common goals, and in turn change the culture of your workplace. In a very real sense, reframing represents a way to make painless communication part of your everyday life, and not just your most difficult conversations. Done well, it can become a cornerstone of a new way for everyone to look at their organization and each other.

CHAPTER 10

Managing the Dialogue: Response and Counter-Response

In an ideal world, you would give people feedback, the recipients of this feedback would appreciate it, and everyone would live happily ever after. Unfortunately, you live on this planet. This means that one of the most important parts of your feedback toolkit is understanding how to respond to objections, criticism, or negativity.

Here as well, our human nature works against us, but the right communications skills can move us from our instinctive stance of "Here is why I am right and you are wrong" to a more authentic one of "I understand and respect how you feel, and here is the issue we need to solve together." This chapter looks at common types of response scenarios, and the mechanics of how to channel them into a productive strength-based dialogue.

BECOMING "INDEFENSIBLE"

Whether we agree with someone or not, the very first thing most of us do in response to other people is usually the very last thing they care about: We defend ourselves. If there is one thing I would like you to learn about responding to people, front and center, it is that *self-defense represents the most fundamental mistake of ineffective dialogue.*

At best, most self-defense statements sound extraneous to others; at worst, they can lead them to feel that you don't "get" what they are trying to tell you, or are even fighting back at them. Compare how the following two statements sound:

> *Defensive:* "You are right, my behavior did inconvenience you, but I'm reacting to everyone else's provocations."
> *Non-Defensive:* "You are right, my behavior did inconvenience you."

See what a difference a few less words make? In the first case, you are making the other person responsible for everyone else's behavior, while the second statement takes ownership and gets to the point of the discussion.

In general, the rule of thumb when you are being attacked is to openly acknowledge the other person's concerns, and assess what they would like (which, because you have read this far, you probably realize is not the same as agreeing with their grievances) in an atmosphere that keeps the dialogue open to troubleshoot the problem. For example:

> **COLLEAGUE:** You didn't give me a chance to speak up at the last meeting.
> **YOU:** I obviously frustrated you about being heard. What could have helped keep this from happening?

> **MANAGER:** This issue wouldn't have become a problem if you had paid attention to it.
> **YOU:** You feel I should have dealt with this a lot earlier. Where can we go from here?

> **EMPLOYEE:** You don't follow the same standards you expect of us.
> **YOU:** So you perceive that there is a double standard. Tell me more.

By keeping an open, nonjudgmental stance toward personal accusations, you not only gather information that helps you troubleshoot the problem, but you also gain more credibility in the eyes of the other person. For example, in the case discussed here about having a double standard, an employee may not realize that you are required to attend numerous off-site management meetings, while everyone else must show up on time. But if you blurt this out as your first response, the other person may see this as an excuse rather than a justification. By addressing her concerns first, you talk *with* each other instead of *past* each other.

Not defending yourself clearly goes against our natural instincts, but in general, the fewer self-protective things you say, the better. That said, here are some of the very few occasions where a little gentle self-defense might make sense:

- When an explanation would make the other person feel better ("I didn't give you a tough assignment to punish you, I gave it to you because I feel you are our best employee.")
- When an explanation would build a better relationship with people ("People may not realize that I've been caring for an ill relative every afternoon, with management's approval, and not just sneaking out early.")
- When the gravity of another person's accusation demands a response ("I believe in healthy competition, but I have honestly never done anything intentionally to undermine another person's sales.")

In general, the rule of thumb is that self-defense should somehow have a clear benefit for the other person, and ultimately, lead both parties toward a resolution. Otherwise, the best approach is to start learning to become "indefensible."

MANAGING SPECIFIC RESPONSES

Now that you understand the importance and the mechanics of responding in a nondefensive manner, let's look at some of the most common situations we might encounter in a difficult workplace conversation. Key types of responses you may hear when you are in the heat of the dialogue include the following:

Anger. The whole point of painless conversation techniques is to prevent anger, and the vast majority of the time this should be the case. That being said, there are situations where people may still react angrily to whatever you say, for a variety of reasons:

- The subject may be a "hot button" issue that stirs up a lot of emotion in the other person no matter how diplomatically it is addressed.

- The other person may feel defensive or threatened by the issue itself, and respond from the mistaken belief that "the best defense is a good offense."
- Some people have a negotiating style where they feel that anger works for them, so it becomes their first recourse.

Challenge. One of the fundamental characteristics of difficult workplace conversations is that the other person may not agree with you—or may not *want* to agree with you, even if you are right. Here are some examples of situations where you may get challenged:

- The other person does not perceive the same behavior or performance problems that you do.
- The other person disagrees with your point of view.
- The other person has a vested interest, no matter how right or wrong you are, in challenging your perceptions.

Blame-Shifting. Another tactic that people often use is that rather than getting upset or challenging you, they make it clear that if it wasn't for George, Sandy, or your management, the problem you describe wouldn't exist. Blame-shifting can be particularly frustrating because when you structure a painless discussion properly, you aren't blaming anyone; rather, you just want the problem resolved.

Mystification. This term, first described by famed psychologist R.D. Laing, describes what happens when people simply deny the reality of what you are saying or shift the focus of the discussion. Unlike shifting the blame, where the problem is real but is perceived to be someone else's fault, the goal of mystification is to make the problem go away by denying its existence. Here are some examples:

- The other person ignores the facts about a problem and insists everything is fine.
- You are concerned over someone's behavior, and the other person replies, "I'll bet you've been under a lot of stress lately and are finding fault with many people."

- You are coaching someone on how to handle a situation better and they reply, "Oh, I do that already"—except that they don't.

Lack of Acknowledgment. Finally, for some people, the best answer is no answer at all. Going silent, ignoring you, or changing the subject can all be thoughtfully chosen verbal weapons that people use when they feel powerless, defensive, or passive-aggressive. Ironically, for many people, the cost of "going ostrich" is often more of the kind of confrontation they fear in the first place.

For each of these types of reactions, the process for how you should respond is very similar to the skills you learned with the CANDID approach:

1. Acknowledge their agenda.
2. Speak to their interests.
3. Focus on the facts, not the emotion, of the situation.

Here are some examples of using this method with each of the situations we just mentioned:

Anger. You discuss someone's productivity and they explode with a raging diatribe about how they have been working here for over 20 years, and how no one had ever worried about their performance until now.

Response:

Acknowledge their concerns: "I can tell by your tone of voice that you are feeling really upset about this."
Speak to their interests: "I am not out to disrespect you. You have been here a long time, and you do have a lot of experience."
Discuss the facts, not the emotions of the situation: "Since we started formally measuring everyone's performance, most people make an average of 20 calls per day, and you make eight. How do you feel we should address this?"

Challenge. You ask someone to start coming in on time and she retorts, "You are just discriminating against me because I have a handicap! I'll bet that you don't pay attention when people who aren't in wheelchairs come in a few minutes late."

Response:

Acknowledge their concerns: "I would be upset if I felt someone was discriminating against me because of a handicap."
Speak to their interests: "You are a good employee and we want you to be successful here."
Discuss the facts, not the emotions of the situation: "We observe you coming in late more frequently than other people, and you have indicated that you do not need any special accommodation to do your job. Where can we go from here?"

Blame-Shifting. Your accounts payable department has come under fire for taking over two months to pay people, as opposed to the normal 30 days. When you try to discuss this with your accounting supervisor, he replies, "The problem is that we are understaffed here!" You do not agree with him.

Response:

Acknowledge their concerns: "You clearly feel overwhelmed by the current volume of work."
Speak to their interests: "I would like to resolve this in a way that is fair to everyone."
Discuss the facts, not the emotions of the situation: "The accounts payable department has an above-average level of staffing relative to the industry, and a below-average response time. Where do you think the problems might break down?"

Mystification. You are talking with your boss about high levels of turnover in your department, which you believe are caused by stress resulting from people's workloads. She responds, "I don't feel you have a turnover problem. When people leave this quickly, they are probably slackers who didn't really want to be here."

Response:

Acknowledge their concerns: "You clearly feel that the quality of people we keep is more important than the number of them who leave."
Speak to their interests: "I certainly don't want to have people on our team who give less than their best either."
Discuss the facts, not the emotions of the situation: "We seem to be losing some of our most productive people lately, and they tell me in exit interviews that they feel unappreciated and overworked. What would you do in my situation?"

Lack of acknowledgment. You try to talk to one of your employees about an interpersonal conflict between her and another peer, which you feel is sapping the energy of your team. She shrugs and says, "I'm not sure what to say about that," and then turns away.

Response:

Acknowledge their concerns: "I realize this may be an uncomfortable situation."
Speak to their interests: "I respect whether you are OK talking about this right now or not."
Discuss the facts, not the emotions of the situation: "Other people on the team are concerned about how the friction between you and Amy is affecting them. I would like to see what I can do to help."

In each of these cases, you are not just answering the other person's responses with grace and respect, but you are also following a very structured process that you can employ all day long if you need to, in order to stay in productive dialogue. It is powerful and it works because it triggers the other person's innate "friend-versus-foe" reflex in your favor by engaging his or her interests. In the process, that uncomfortable feeling of "what will this person say next" can be replaced by the confidence of knowing exactly how to respond to anyone in any situation.

THE GRADUATE COURSE: DEALING WITH SPECIFIC PERSONALITIES

So far, we have discussed examples of responses that could erupt as a result of a situation, the other person's reaction, or both. But what about those people whose personalities are likely to color their response to *any* situation? An important part of your toolkit is understanding how to deal productively with personality issues that can stand in the way of effective, productive communication.

Here we will look at specific techniques for interacting with these personalities, techniques that work in concert with the CANDID technique and productive response strategies.

The Critic. Everyone disagrees with some things some of the time, but the critic is someone who constantly begs to differ; it is a fundamental part of her strategy for dealing with others. Often seen by others as a nitpicker and a fault-finder, the critic will poke holes in your logic, question your competence, and have extremely high standards for everyone else. Constant critics generally feel the need to be "one up" on others, and their gripes frequently stem from a sense of insecurity about their own mediocrity. Here are some productive ways for dealing with the critic:

- *Thank them for their feedback.* Many people feel that by acknowledging a critic, they are encouraging more of the same behavior. I gently disagree with this view. In my experience, the more common scenario is when critics feel ignored, they push back harder to be heard. By acknowledging and appreciating a critic, you become less of a target yourself.
- *Validate their concerns.* The advice in this chapter for acknowledging and validating another person's concerns applies even more so to critics, because of their sensitivity. Be sure to use plenty of both in your responses.
- *Limit self-defensive responses.* Critics love to challenge people's defenses, so don't provide them in the first place. Keep your responses to clear, factual, and constructive statements. If at all possible, never volunteer them first.
- *Use the "opportunity cost" technique.* When critics want you to change things, put them to work! Ask them to show you what they would like in the future, and have them invest their time and energy

in developing alternatives. When critics feel that their concerns might create more work for themselves, they are much more likely to think twice before they challenge you.

The Joker. In school, most of us grew up with someone who was the class clown. For a much smaller number of people in adult life, class is seemingly in session for perpetuity. Jokers are people who will not give a serious answer to anything, would rather make quips than engage in productive dialogue, and frequently like to make fun of you and others. Jokers are often but not always male, and they tend to respond imperviously to criticism with a sarcastic, "Can't you take a joke?" Here are some ways to respond to a joker:

- *If the humor is simply annoying, acknowledge it first.* Making a comment such as, "That's a good one, Steve" gives the joker the recognition he expects while setting the stage to move on. As with the critic, following common wisdom to simply ignore the joker can in reality be much more likely to cause defensiveness and hostility, often in the form of cutting humor.
- *If the humor is inappropriate, set boundaries without criticism.* Statements such as, "I respect you and appreciate being treated with respect in return" make it clear that you will honor your own boundaries without humiliating the joker or putting him on the defensive.
- *Don't fight back, but it is OK to respond in kind.* How comfortable are you with your own sense of humor? If the answer is "not very," do not try to match wits with the joker because the results may appear forced and awkward. But if you can match him at his game, a little give-and-take establishes you as a peer and demonstrates acceptance.
- *Gently and politely keep things on topic.* As with any dialogue, the key in moving forward with a joker is to keep acknowledging him—at first verbally, and perhaps later with what are known as "minimal encourages" such as smiling or nodding—and following this up with polite, factual, on-topic discussion.

The Negotiator. Nearly everyone argues for what they want, in any discussion. With the negotiator, however, nothing you propose is ever good enough. They value being right as much as they value getting what they want, and they keep trying to wear you down in search of a better deal. Perhaps the most obvious difference between negotiators and others is that while most people push for things in specific situations, the negotiator is showing a predictable personality style. Here is how to deal with it:

- *Acknowledge and validate their wants.* Making statements that acknowledge a pushy negotiator can feel like walking straight into the fire. But ironically, the more detailed and authentic your acknowledgment is, the more power you take away from the negotiator because you have preempted them from arguing much of their case. Saying things like, "I realize how badly you want to go on this business trip because you feel it will be a good personal development opportunity" are great if you can accommodate them, but even greater when you feel you cannot. This is because you remove all doubt in this person's mind that you do not understand him.
- *Respond with what you can do.* Most people are focused on defending why they cannot accommodate a negotiator, but I want you to focus instead on how your preferred solution can benefit him. When someone demands the moon and the stars, it feels funny to be offering half a moon and part of a star. But if this is all you can legitimately offer him, the language of benefiting someone is tremendously powerful.
- *Repeat as needed.* This is perhaps the key point of dealing with a negotiator, and it borrows from an age-old principle of psychological self-help known as "fogging." The idea is that people quickly stop throwing bricks at a fogbank that does not respond to them.[1] Keep acknowledging the negotiator, explain the situation empathetically, and most important, keep using the magic phrases "I wish" and "even though" to transition back to what you *can* do (for example, "I wish I could send you on this business trip, but even though there is currently no budget for this, I can give you an afternoon off to do some research on this at the local university"). More often than not, the other person will give up following the second or third go-around.

The Distancer. This person seeks power by limiting access and being a gatekeeper for whatever information or access they control. She tends to avoid direct conflict versus cutting people out of the communication loop and giving people the silent treatment. People who use distancing as a personality style frequently find themselves in positions of power but not authority—for example, an executive assistant or a person in charge of access to a database—and use this power to assert authority in their own way. Here is how to deal with a distancer:

- *Openly respect their time, space, and power.* When you acknowledge the distancer's position, using statements like, "I appreciate how critical you are to this process," or "I want to make sure we go through the proper channels," you remove an important source of challenge and conflict early in the transaction.
- *Use "negative option" phrasing.* Where possible, frame things in terms of what you will do in the absence of a distancer's cooperation ("I am going to do X, unless you have any objections") to remove the element of waiting on the distancer for a resolution as much as possible. The reason this is effective is that actively taking steps to block you is normally more awkward or involved than simply saying "no" or making you wait.
- *Go slowly and validate their responses.* With a distancer, force or pressure is your worst option. In general, the harder you push, the more they tend to withdraw or block you. Your best chance of success with a distancer lies in rolling with her style of communication and respecting her role and then making a neutral and factual case for what you want.

There are several common threads through each of these situations. First of all, there is a process to engaging in more productive dialogue with specific personalities. Second, a painless approach that involves acknowledgment, validation, and respect generally makes it easier to honor your own boundaries, not harder. Many people do not recognize that you can stand your ground and understand the other person at the same time because it goes against our nature. But when you start making this a habit, many so-called personality conflicts start melting away in the face of simply using better communications skills.

This, in turn, leads us to what is perhaps the key point in responding to other people: You ultimately get more of what you want by making it all about them. When you move past self-defense and move toward a process of actively listening and responding to people's concerns, you take our most common sources of conflict off the table and move closer to the heart of consensus. Combined with painless techniques for raising issues in the first place, such as the CANDID process, this style of response will confidently put you in the driver's seat of most workplace discussions.

NOTE

1. Manuel J. Smith, *When I Say No, I Feel Guilty* (New York: Bantam, 1985).

CHAPTER 11

You Don't Say:
Phrases to Avoid

ords are funny things. We assign meanings to them. We put them in dictionaries. And then we go ahead and use them in ways that have nothing to do with these original meanings. And even more amazing, many of us actually think that we are communicating clearly when we do! Take a look at some of these examples:

- A man angrily says, "I'm sorry, but you aren't going to do that!" Is he conveying any regret?
- A woman says, "Excuse me, but what were you thinking?" Is she excusing herself?
- You complain about something to a disengaged customer service agent who wearily nods, "I understand, sir." Does he, in fact, understand?
- You ask your boss for a raise, and she replies, "We'll see." How much money would you like to wager on the likelihood that she will, in fact, see about it?
- When Rhett Butler told Scarlett O'Hara ,"Frankly, my dear . . ." at the end of the movie *Gone With the Wind*, was he attempting to endear her with his frankness?

We could go on, but you get the point. We have a uniquely human trait of taking phrases that were originally designed to be helpful and using them in ways that will tick people off. And the reason that many people get angry in these situations—as well as the reason that many of *your* efforts at difficult conversations are often doomed to failure—lies in the cultural context of how we have learned to react to certain phrases.

An important aspect of creating painless discussions is learning to avoid common phrases that are extremely counterproductive to effective dialogue. These are phrases that you don't say if you want to succeed, many of which have become ingrained within the average person's vocabulary.

This chapter looks at the most ineffective phrases that people often use in giving people feedback, explains the dynamics of what happens when you use them, and then shares some very powerful and productive new ways to express the same ideas.

THE PSYCHOLOGY OF THE CATCH PHRASE

Why, given that we are all presumably nice people, do we say things that not only do not help our cause, but are in fact likely to set people against us? The answer lies in how catch phrases come into existence in the first place.

According to the dictionary, a catch phrase is "an expression that has caught on and is used repeatedly." These phrases often begin life with a good or at least benign purpose. For example, the first people to say, "I understand" probably really *did* understand, and the phrase, "I'm sorry" was first intended as a sincere gesture of apology. Before they become catch phrases, these newly hatched expressions generally have the legitimate intention of being polite, showing respect, or softening the blow of a difficult message.

But then something amazing happens. As more and more people use these phrases, soon their very commonality creates more distance than comfort. So, for example, the honest and well-intentioned "I have no idea" becomes a code phrase for telling someone to buzz off and stop bothering them. Sometimes a phrase even intentionally evolves through sarcasm to become its antonym. For example, the popular saying "let's do lunch" that originated in the Los Angeles entertainment industry is now often used to mean "get lost."

More darkly, a catch phrase can also be intentionally confrontational, particularly if it is shocking or funny. No one would laugh if television cartoon character Bart Simpson said, "I would rather not do this," but we all laugh when he says, "Eat my shorts!" And soon, this phrase became part of our culture. Sometimes blunt expressions also begin life with the intention of being humorous or even protective. For example, telling your child, "Forget about it!"

could underscore how strongly you feel about him doing something unsafe. But here as well, these phrases often evolve with time and repetitive use, to the point that they end up pushing people away and putting them on the defensive, when in fact most of us simply want to reach consensus with others.

So how do we stop letting our language get in the way of our real intentions? The simple answer is to stop using catch phrases entirely. At the same time, they have become so ingrained within our language and culture that the act of going through even a single day without them can seem Herculean. And getting through your most difficult conversations without them can make you feel as exposed and vulnerable as answering the doorbell in your pajamas.

That is where this chapter comes in. In the next few pages, we are going to have fun looking at some of our most common catch phrases, what really happens when you say them, and more important, what you can say instead to become a much more effective communicator.

Brutal Honesty

When we are giving people feedback, perhaps the most common types of toxic catch phrases we use involve giving "honest" feedback. I call these kinds of phrases "brutal honesty" because too often they are more brutal than honest. Here are some of the most common examples.

"Let me be totally honest about this."

You don't, in fact, need another person's permission to be honest about something. In fact, it is a good idea to be honest with people most of the time, unless perhaps your five-year-old is asking, "Dad, where do babies come from?" Yet many of us still feel compelled to use this phrase because we think it will get someone's attention. More to the point, we think it will serve as a euphemistic way of telling someone, "Your idea stinks," or "What you asked for isn't going to happen."

This phrase does actually accomplish both of these goals, at a cost of putting the other person in a one-down position and getting them frustrated. It is a genteel way of saying, "I know better than you" in a way that is completely obvious to both the speaker and the listener. In the process, you are distancing yourself in a way that reduces, rather than enhances, your influence and credibility.

Once we get past the linguistics of this statement and start looking at its hidden meaning, we run into an even thornier problem. Have you ever heard someone say, "Let me be totally honest about this" and then follow it by telling you how great you are? Probably not. And therein lies the real problem: It prepares the listener for the fact that you are about to criticize him, which in turn will instantly put him on the defensive—which explains why this phrase is never, ever followed by the listener saying, "Golly, thank you for your honesty!"

What you can say instead: The intended purpose of this phrase is twofold: to get the other person's attention and to disabuse them of what they were thinking. You can accomplish the same goals much more effectively through a two-step process of (a) validating what the other person is thinking, and then (b) selling the benefits of your approach. Let's compare these two approaches:

Not so good:
"Let me be totally honest with you. Trading futures in horse manure is not a good strategic direction for our company."

Better:
"It sounds like you are thinking creatively about how biofuels might add to our trading portfolio. Let me walk you through what I'm thinking, as there might be some other areas that have even more growth potential than horse manure."

"I hate to tell you this."

As with the previous phrase, the expression "I hate to tell you this" serves as an early warning signal to the other person that he or she is about to be criticized or put on the defensive. This, in turn, makes it less likely that you will get what you want. More important, this phrase accomplishes something that good negotiators tell you never to do: It tips your hand. By telling someone that you hate to say what is to follow, you are alerting them, at least technically, that you are about to say something you are uncomfortable with.

The roots of this phrase lie in the best of intentions, at several levels. At one level, you are trying to prepare them for bad news, which is always a good goal. (However, this is not the way to do it.) At another level, it represents an attempt to personalize the message by sharing your feelings and concern. Perhaps most important, you are trying to soften the blow of the bad news that follows by making it clear that you take no joy or comeuppance in sharing it. At the same time, this catch phrase now has a history behind it that undermines each of these noble goals and simply makes you sound like a remorseless critic and bearer of bad news.

What to say instead: The best approach in this situation involves the *reframing* technique we discussed in Chapter 9, where you change the frame of reference from what is bad about a situation to what is good, hopeful, or possible. For example:

- Instead of telling people they are doing a bad job, tell them what standards they could meet to help them do a good job.
- Instead of telling them that something isn't acceptable, let them know what will work better.
- Instead of telling them that they need to change something, show them how they will benefit.

Here is an example of how you can reframe this phrase:

Before:
"I hate to tell you this, but I don't think you are promotable."

After:
"I can see very clearly what kinds of things would make you promotable in the future."

"I am telling you this for your own good."

This is a phrase that has its roots in what people say to their small children to protect them from hidden danger, such as why they shouldn't play with matches. In all likelihood, this argument doesn't impress your kids very much. When you use it with grown men and women in the workplace, it is even less effective. Allow me to translate how this phrase is interpreted by the listener: "You are too stupid to know what is best for you, even when it comes to your own interests, so I am going to try to impose my will on you."

The impact of these words is then further complicated by the relationship you have with the listener. If you are a peer with this person, the assumption that you need to tell them what to do comes across as patronizing and supercilious. If you don't have a direct working relationship with the listener, it carries the sense of sticking your nose where it doesn't belong. Perhaps most important, if you are this person's supervisor, it conveys a value judgment about the listener that poisons the working relationship, long after the original issue has been resolved.

What to say instead: Most of the time, people say, "I am telling you this for your own good" because you and the listener disagree about a course of action. Moreover, it usually gets uttered when there is already a certain level of distrust and contention between the two of you.

This means that your first opportunity to convince the other person using just the beauty of your logic has passed and will never again return. Therefore, your best hope of influencing them now lies in making it clear that you understand how they feel, so validating the argument first is far and away the best way to share your own opinion. For example:

You: "I can see why you want to do things that way. I just wanted to share some thoughts on how things have gone for me in the past, which might benefit you."

Ultimately, instead of telling people things "for their own good," you will normally get much more mileage by finding the other person's greater good and speaking to it directly. As long as you acknowledge how this person is thinking first, you are much more likely to have respect and legitimacy in the other person's mind.

"That is a no-brainer."

People often use the phrase "that's a no-brainer" to emphasize that a particular course of action is the logical one; in other words, that no thinking effort is needed to come to this conclusion.

If two people already agree on something, it can be a benign phrase of affirmation for both parties. But this phrase is also a potential minefield that can be extremely derogatory for anyone who has a different opinion:

- If the other person carefully weighed the alternatives and thoughtfully chose to do something else, telling her that the decision you made is a "no-brainer" invalidates much of her decision-making process.
- If someone else has not yet made up his mind, telling him that one choice is a "no-brainer" pressures him to see things your way, which at best makes you seem closed-minded, and at worst, a bully.
- When someone actually sees things differently from you, labeling your view as a "no-brainer" puts her in the awkward and embarrassing position of either contradicting you or remaining silent.

- When a person has already voiced an opposing opinion, calling the alternative a "no-brainer" represents an extremely humiliating insult; you are accusing them of not being capable of thinking.

What to say instead. It is OK to disagree with people, and it is also OK to produce evidence to support these disagreements. It is not OK to belittle another person's opinions or choices, however. Instead of calling something a "no-brainer," consider these alternatives:

- *Acknowledge, validate, respond.* Give the other person credit for their opinions, and then share yours from a standpoint of mutual respect. For example, "I can see why you don't want your team to do this project. You are all very busy. Let's lay out what everyone's workloads look like from here and see what makes the most sense for everyone."

- *Seek the benefit.* If something is a "no-brainer" in your mind because it has a positive impact on the other person, frame your response that way. For example, "There is another alternative that might save you even more money. Here are some of the details about it."

- *Just the facts.* Even if you truly believe the other person's idea is a bad idea, stick to the facts about it without passing a value judgment. For example, "Let's look at the potential impact of this option on our future sales. Other companies who tried this have seen a 17 percent drop in sales."

Catch-Phrase Me if You Can

The next few statements in our rogues' gallery involve catch phrases that on their face seem helpful, except for one small thing: People almost universally react badly to them. Let's look at some of the more common offenders.

"I understand."

No, you don't. When you tell someone that you "understand," you are actually distancing yourself from the other person. This isn't your fault. Rather, it is the fault of years of people using this phrase in contexts like the following:

- "I understand, but I am still not going to let you do what you want."
- "I understand. I am not going to acknowledge anything you say in detail; I am just going to mouth the phrase 'I understand' until you go away and leave me alone."
- "I understand, even though I don't have a clue about what you are talking about and can't be bothered to ask you for more details."

In other words, "I understand" has quickly become a code phrase for "I don't care and I don't want to hear any more details about it. I just want to move on." Which is really a shame because it is often the most common, knee-jerk phrase that even nice people say when another person is unhappy about something.

Of course, *really* understanding another person is a very good thing. That is why it is too bad that "I understand" had to be hijacked as a catch phrase many years ago. So your goal here is to show that you actually do understand—in other words, that you realize how the other person feels and respect it—without resorting to the dreaded two-word rejoinder.

What to say instead. You are in luck with this particular phrase because there is absolutely nothing wrong with the sentiment behind it . The problem is in the way other people process the two words. So literally any other phrase that expresses the same sentiments, in a positive and authentic manner, will work just fine instead. Here are some good examples:

- *"I can see/I can tell."* Here, you are conveying the same sentiments as "I understand," with the key difference that you are not using the catch phrase. More important, you are phrasing things in terms of your own perception, by sharing that you are observing what this person is feeling. This, in turn, shows much more empathy to him or her.

- *"You must be . . ."* In this case, you make a reasonable presumption of how the other person feels, and share it with her. For example, you might say to a stressed coworker, "You must be really upset about that," or "You must be feeling a lot of pressure right now." People sometimes resist using statements like this for fear that they are guessing wrong about the other person's feelings. But ironically, an educated guess is normally well received, even if the listener corrects you about her feelings. (As an aside, crisis counselors are often trained to share their best judgment about a caller's feelings because of the level of empathy it shows.) Use this wording when the other person is reasonably transparent about how something affects him or her and you want to validate it.

- *"I have experienced the same thing and felt the same way."* The true dictionary definition of "understand" revolves around its component words to *stand under*—in other words, you have already stood under what the other person is experiencing. When you use your own genuine, authentic experience to connect with another person, you are using one of the most powerful ways possible to show your understanding.

Of course, as we have discussed throughout this book, acknowledging feelings and experiences is *not* the same as agreeing with the other person's position. When someone expresses that you make people work too hard, and you agree that you hate to feel overworked yourself, it is not the same as agreeing to cut back the other person's workload; it is simply a starting point for productive dialogue. Likewise, when you reflect on how frustrated another person must be at having to do something over, it does not absolve him from his obligations. Showing real understanding is one of the most inexpensive and yet powerful responses to any negative emotion.

"I'm sorry"

Guess what: I want you to banish the term "I'm sorry" from your vocabulary from now on. Forever.

Now I do want you to be apologetic when something has gone wrong. I just want you to stop using this two-word catch phrase that has perhaps caused more anger, frustration, and misunderstanding than any other. To show you what I mean, let's look at how "I'm sorry" is most commonly used by people:

- *The "Yeah, But."* What is the most common word that follows the phrase "I'm sorry"? Of course, it is "but." Far and away, the most frequent use of this phrase is to set limits on people, in situations like the ones below:

"I'm sorry, but you can't join this project team."
"I'm sorry, but I can't help you with this."
"I'm sorry, but that really offends me."

Linguistically, the phrase "I'm sorry" is meant to imply, "Even though I am setting limits or expressing anger, I do regret it." The problem is, most of us don't think linguistically. Today, most people process this phrase as a vainglorious attempt to excuse oneself from the consequences of the rest of the statement, which has just one result: It makes the listener angrier.

• *The Kiss-Off.* How many times have you had a conversation with a disengaged service agent that goes something like this?

You: My month-old computer just died with a hard drive crash! My business is at a standstill!

Service Agent: Sir, I am sorry this has happened to you.

You: Good! Does this mean you will refund my money?

Service Agent: I didn't say that, sir. Our policy is that after the first 14 days we perform repairs only.

You: Being without my computer for very long is going to cost me a lot of money.

Service Agent: I am sorry for your inconvenience, sir.

You: Sorry enough that you will fix this immediately?

Service Agent: I didn't say that, sir. Our response is six weeks for repairs.

Now, wasn't that exchange just oozing with remorse? You are right, it wasn't. So what kind of impact do you think these scripted "I'm sorry" statements have on you as a customer? Right again. They make you even angrier.

• *The Insincere Apology.* Finally, some people use "I'm sorry" for its intended purpose, which is to express regret when something goes wrong. Unfortunately, its status as a catch phrase makes it one of the most ineffective ways to express regret, compared with a more detailed discussion of how you feel and what you will do about the situation.

What to say instead: Just like with "I understand," literally any wording that expresses sincere remorse while avoiding the catch phrase "I'm sorry" will generally work much better at connecting with people. Try these on for size:

"I wish that hadn't happened to you."

"I feel badly that you had to go through that."

"I would like to do what we can to make this situation right."

Finally, avoid at all costs the use of "I'm sorry" to soften the blow of bad news. Instead, use the techniques in this book to word things with respect and dignity to the other person, and speak to their interests. Here is one example:

Not so good:

"I'm sorry, but I can't send you to this conference."

Better:

"I wish I could send you to this conference. Let's look at some other options."

The phrase "I'm sorry" is so firmly ingrained in our culture, with all of its good and bad uses, that you will probably find it to be one of the hardest ones to personally give up. When you succeed, however, the difference it makes in effective dialogue will be truly remarkable.

"We'll see."

Taken literally, the phrase "we'll see" implies that you will look into something. In reality, it means "don't hold your breath about this," or more simply "no." If someone is in fact waiting for you to see about something after you use this phrase, she could be in for a very long wait.

The roots of using this phrase go back to our human nature, which often seeks to avoid the confrontation that might follow by simply saying no. By using a euphemistic term like "we'll see," we feel we are buying ourselves time and space for the issue to simply go away. Many of us remember being told this phrase by our parents when we were growing up, particularly when they were too tired to fight with us.

Unfortunately, there is one problem with this logic. This catch phrase has become so ingrained in our consciousness that most people now process it as "no." Worse, it leaves the infuriating sense that you are not being totally frank with the other person, which can lead to hard feelings and more conflict. Ultimately, it makes you come across as insincere and uncooperative.

What to say instead: There is a passage in the Bible that reads, "Let your yes be yes and your no be no."[1] I would take this a step further: Let your yes be your yes, and your no turn into a dialogue focused on what you can do for the other person. Compare these two examples:

Not so good:
CHESTER: We are going to be moving to a new floor soon. Can I have the corner office?
YOU *(knowing that Chester is a relatively junior employee)*: We'll see.

Better:
CHESTER: We are going to be moving to a new floor soon. Can I have the corner office?
YOU: I would like to see everyone be happy with the space they are in when we move. Given that we usually select offices by seniority, what kinds of things do you feel are important for your workspace?

In a very real sense, avoiding the term "we'll see" not only keeps you from using a frustrating catch phrase, but it also forces you to adopt the discipline of giving thoughtful, strength-based responses to other people's questions, even when the answer is not what they want to hear. Therefore, learning to drop this phrase from your vocabulary can have a very immediate and positive impact on the honesty and authenticity of your communications with others.

Avoid Making Your "No" as Negative as Possible

"I have no idea."
"Forget about it."
"That is a stupid idea."
"I can't believe that you brought this up."

When someone asks you to do something, you normally have two choices: you will say yes or you will say no. Normally, if you are trying to make people feel good, you would make your "yeses" as enthusiastic as possible and your "no's" as diplomatic as possible; as Dale Carnegie once recommended, you would "be hearty in your approbation and lavish in your praise."[2] Unfortunately, we usually do exactly the opposite of this. Why is that?

The answer is self-protection — or more accurately, a misguided sense of self-protection. We think that by minimizing a "yes" answer we avoid being seen as weak and easily taken advantage of, and by maximizing our "no," we appear strong, decisive, and not to be trifled with.

Drilling down a little deeper, these reactions spring from the fear that if we don't put up a good offense at first, we will be in the uncomfortable position of being pressured to do something we don't want. We lack confidence in our ability to manage other people's demands so we do our best to simply prevent them. Like animals protecting their turf or their offspring, we feel that we must bare our teeth first to defend ourselves.

So how effective is this technique? Just think about how you felt the last time someone talked like that to you. You probably thought that this person was being a rude jerk. And to add insult to injury, you were probably *more* likely to fight for what you wanted with this person, not less. This is why minimizing your "no" answers — or better yet, avoiding "no" entirely by reframing the discussion — is a very important skill for painless communication with others.

What to say instead: When you are tempted to say "no" to someone, focus instead on what you *can* acknowledge and what you *can* do. A key to painless dialogue is turning "no's" into understanding and alternatives. Here are some examples:

Not so good:
ANGELINA: I would like some more time off this month.
YOU: Forget about it. This is our busy season.

Better:
ANGELINA: I would like some more time off this month.
YOU: Let's discuss what you want. We have lots of availability for vacation time in just a few weeks.

Not so good:
VICTOR: I feel I deserve a raise.
YOU: I can't believe you want a raise already. You've only been here six months.

Better:
Victor: I feel I deserve a raise.
You: Let's talk about it. Where do you feel you are adding more value nowadays?

Not so good:
Samir: Do you know the address of our subcontractor?
You: I have no idea.

Better:
Samir: Do you know the address of our subcontractor?
You: I wish I did. You might check with our accounting department.

In each of these cases, you lower the heat entirely by avoiding the negative catch phrase while still being honest with the other person about what they are asking. By learning to focus on what is possible instead of simply setting limits, you take much of the sting out of what you cannot do for other people.

Waving Red Flags in Front of Bulls

"You'll have to."
"You can't."
"So what do you expect?"
"Don't hold your breath."

What is the quickest way to start a fight with your three-year-old? Tell him that he cannot do something. Next question: What is the quickest way to start a fight with your 33-year-old coworker, or your entire team of employees? Ditto.

Throughout history, putting limits on other people has not only been a flash point of contention, but also a powerful motivating force for change. Whether it was Elvis Presley being told he would never succeed as a singer, or Germans banding together to take down the Berlin Wall, many things have their roots in people being told that they cannot do things. Unfortunately, this powerful force works against you when you are the person trying to set the boundaries.

There is some interesting psychology going on from both sides when you set limits with people. On your end, it is often tempting to be more aggressive and use phrases like the ones above so that it leaves no doubt of our intentions in the other person's mind. Does it work? Sure it does—some of the time. But on the other side of the transaction, people hearing these messages always react negatively, even if they simply fume and walk away. This is because it triggers some of our most basic instincts about being challenged or threatened.

An even more interesting point is that the harder we push, the stronger the reaction, which sometimes leads people to fight back *even when they did not want something in the first place*. When you are too aggressive about setting boundaries, this can often change the game from one of seeking permission to one of defending one's honor. This is why, when you feel the need to put constraints on another person's behavior, you need to think less like an enforcer and more like a diplomat.

What to say instead: Ultimately, the most powerful way to keep someone from doing something is to get them to acknowledge that it cannot be done rather than you doing it. This means that instead of aggressively setting limits, you should *acknowledge feelings* and *share facts*, so that the other person can make a logical response. For example:

Not so good:
"You can't just barge in on senior executives with your ideas."

Better:
"I don't blame you for wanting a high-level audience for your ideas. Senior executives are often hard to reach, and it is difficult to get their attention. I wonder if there are other channels that might be more effective."

Not so good:
"What do you expect, after missing the meeting? It's too late to take a lead role now."

Better:
"You want to get up to speed as quickly as you can, seeing as you missed the meeting. Let's look at where you can go from here."

Not so good:
"You'll have to fill out this paperwork first."

Better:
"Once you complete this paperwork, we can get you started right away."

In each of these cases, you are replacing "can't" language with information that treats the listener as an intelligent person capable of making his or her own decisions, while still making your own preferences clear. You are replacing pushback with productive dialogue, and more often than not, a mutual consensus on what can or cannot be done.

Be Careful What You Discourage

What would you say if one of your college-age sons told you that he wanted to make a living as a poet when he grew up? If you are like many parents, you might launch into a frank discussion of what kinds of odds he would face, liberally peppered with "can't" phrases designed to educate him about reality.

So did you realize that some people actually do make a full-time living as a poet? One man reportedly goes around the country giving poetry readings and selling his books from a stockpile in the trunk of his car. At another level, nationally known poet Maya Angelou has been described as being a millionaire. All of this means that before you open your mouth to respond, you should think carefully about how you would like your son the millionaire poet to think of you years from now.

Discouragement has been around for as long as success has, and many of the world's greatest successes were told their dreams were impossible. Fred Smith, the CEO of shipping giant FedEx, was given a "C" on the graduate school paper that first described its business model by a professor who curtly noted that it would never work. Likewise, the late John Lennon of the Beatles was once told by his aunt, "The guitar's all very well as a hobby, John, but you'll never make a living out of it."[3] So while appropriate cautions are fine, think twice before you open your mouth and become a dream killer. You never know where the energy and interests of other people might lead them.

The way people respond to catch phrases ultimately drives home the key point of this book, which is that the words you use are critically important—sometimes even much more important than the situation itself. The common element between many catch phrases is that most of them spring from early efforts to soften the blow of difficult conversations. But because we are all pretty smart at interpreting what we hear and the intentions behind it, these phrases now often have exactly the opposite effect from their original intentions.

Time and again, you will hear people saying things like, "I did everything I could, but I couldn't reason with him," or "I tried my very best to make her feel better, but she wouldn't hear of it." When a difficult conversation isn't working the way you want it to, take a step back and check your language. I will wager that there are catch phrases lurking among your words, and you may be inadvertently sabotaging yourself.

This is why becoming free of catch phrases is such a powerful tool for painless conversation. Be aware that catch phrases are so strongly ingrained in our culture that no one, including myself, ever avoids them 100 percent of the time. But when you make a thoughtful and purposeful effort to stop using them, the difference will be amazing. It forces you to think, plan, and be authentic with the people you interact with instead of simply answering them on autopilot. Make it a habit, and your dialogues with people will soon have a grace and credibility they never had before.

NOTES

1. *The Holy Bible*, English Standard Version, James 5:12.

2. Dale Carnegie, *How to Win Friends and Influence People* (*Anniversary Edition*) (New York: Pocket Books, 1998).

3. Rock and Roll Hall of Fame, "John Lennon," http://www.rockhall.com/inductee/john-lennon/.

CHAPTER 12

How to Receive Feedback

S o far we have spent a great deal of time examining how to say difficult things to other people as painlessly as possible. But what happens when people have difficult things to say to you? How do you react to them, and how do these discussions turn out?

Try an experiment sometime: Watch a political debate on television and pay attention to what happens when one candidate criticizes another one. In all likelihood, you will hear an exchange something like this:

Candidate A: My opponent has never seen a tax increase she didn't like!

Candidate B: Actually, I fight for what the people want, unlike my opponent here who just wants to cut back all of your services!

Of course, neither of these candidates is exactly using strength-based communication. But there is an even more interesting dynamic going on here as well. These supposedly mature adults could literally spend all day hurling accusations at each other, and neither person would *ever* acknowledge the validity of *any* of them. If this debate went on for hours, you would find that each candidate would have a seemingly superhuman, inexhaustible supply of self-defensive statements and countercharges. And you would probably have long since changed the channel from it.

Now let's move from politics to real life. Think of the last time you really wanted someone to change something that bothered you and you simply came out and told them so. Did they politely agree to change or did they react like these politicians, just defending themselves and hurling countercharges back at you? Many if not most of you probably had the latter experience, and if you did, it was pretty annoying, right? You probably came away from that discussion wondering why people can't just learn from your well-intentioned words of wisdom and simply do the right thing.

Finally, please bear with me as we move into more sensitive personal territory. What happened the last time someone criticized *you* for something? Did you simply acknowledge and agree with them? Or was your response, shall we say, more like someone running for office? Some of you may have been sufficiently egoless to respond neutrally to the facts of the situation, but for many of us, our responses probably sounded rather similar to a presidential debate.

In this chapter, we are going to look at an important but underappreciated aspect of feedback: what *you* say when someone gives *you* some feedback, particularly when what you are hearing isn't exactly painless. When you learn how to react constructively to the things people tell you, especially in sensitive or difficult situations, you do much more than make the other person feel better; you make a fundamental change in your own level of influence and leadership.

BLINDERS AND HIDDEN BIASES: RECOGNIZING OUR OWN RESPONSE TO FEEDBACK

Remember how we talked earlier in this book about how human beings instinctively get defensive when they are criticized no matter how "right" this criticism was? Well, guess what? You are a human being. And if you are like most human beings, you have probably reacted to other people's feedback in ways that didn't exactly promote good will and harmony. If so, you are far from alone. You can count yourself among a large fraternity that includes psychologists, clergy, senior corporate executives, and nearly every person who has ever appeared on a television talk show. It is, in a very real sense, the last taboo of effective communication.

The key thing you will learn here is responding effectively to another person's feedback is much like giving it. It requires learning specific procedural skills, rather than just trying to achieve sainthood. It is a structured process that anyone can master, and that gets better with practice. But first, let's take a look at what normally happens when someone gives us feedback. Normally, it is a three-step process that goes something like this:

1. Someone makes a simple, factual statement. For example, "You have a piece of lettuce stuck between your teeth."

2. In less than a split second, you *translate* this sentence to what it means to you. For example:
   - "She is always trying to show me up!"
   - "The nerve of this woman, who can barely put together a matching outfit, telling me how I look!"
   - "Uh-oh, I must re-establish my competence in the eyes of this person."
   - "Golly, I have a piece of lettuce stuck between my teeth."

3. We respond to the *translation*, not the original statement, with a response that could be:
   - A snippy comeback. For example, "How nice of you to be my personal coach."
   - A hasty excuse such as," I was just on my way to the restroom to floss my teeth."
   - Stony silence.
   - A simple "thank you."

The great Albert Ellis, widely regarded as the father of modern cognitive-behavioral psychology, referred to this as a process of forming *irrational beliefs*, using terms such as "awfulizing" or "can't-stand-it-itis" to describe how we respond to situations like these. Today, addressing these irrational beliefs has become fundamental to how therapists treat emotional problems, and it also represents the key to transforming how we respond to feedback. So let's look at some of the reasons that we all naturally engage in this process.

We have emotional "blinders" that affect what we hear. There is an old saying that when you are a hammer, everything looks like a nail. In much the same way, the concerns at the top of our minds act as a filter to everything we hear from people. For example:

- When you are a manager, someone's feedback may seem like an affront to your authority whether it was actually meant that way or not.
- When you are a precise, exacting technologist, an innocent suggestion may seem like an attack on your perfectionism.

- When you are very feeling-oriented, a factual critique can easily (and mistakenly) be interpreted as a judgment of you as a person.

We each see the world differently from other people. Each of us has subtle biases that affect how we interpret other people and the messages they send us. For example:

- Someone may be asking you for more detail and you might be writing them off as a "nitpicker."
- Feedback about how you could improve something may go against your ideas about what a subordinate should be saying to their boss.
- Someone may wish we cared more about people, while we feel that people should "suck it up" and get back to work.

We have a strong, innate urge to protect ourselves. Whenever anyone says anything critical of us, it is instinctive for each of us to CYA (cover your analysis). This is not necessarily because we are egotists or defensive, but rather because we are all strongly programmed to feel this way as a survival instinct. As a result:

- When someone points out a shortcoming, we immediately produce an excuse (real or imagined) for it.
- When someone is upset with us about something, we often counter with our grievances about the other person.
- When someone wants us to improve, we focus on the validity of their complaint rather than what we can change.

All of these instincts kick in to even higher gear the more upset or critical another person is. As a result, we are very hard people to criticize! This is why most of us need to learn a structured process for being on the receiving end of a difficult conversation, just like we do for initiating one. So let's look at one such approach and start changing our natural defense mechanisms into productive dialogue.

Responding to Difficult Conversations: The PLAN Approach

When someone starts a challenging conversation with you, human nature is not your best friend. At the same time, most of us cannot learn to respond effectively to these situations on the fly, when the other person's agenda is hurtling toward you like a runaway freight train. This is why you need more than good intentions to respond effectively to other people: you need a plan.

So I have a PLAN for you. It is a four-step process that puts your response completely and painlessly on autopilot. Here are the steps:

- *Paraphrase* what the other person is saying to you.
- *Listen* for their response.
- *Acknowledge* what they are saying.
- *Negotiate* a resolution.

Each of these steps is simple, logical, and precisely the opposite of what we normally do in a difficult dialogue. At the same time, once you get used to using them, you will become amazed at how comfortable you are with anything that another person could possibly say to you. Let's explore each of these steps in detail.

Step 1: Paraphrase

When someone gives you feedback—particularly critical feedback—do you feel at a sudden loss for words? Or worse, primed to fight back? Then this step will take a big load off your mind because the first thing you should say in response requires almost no creativity whatsoever. In fact, you will use a simple, mechanical process that is more powerful than any clever response you could come up with: You will simply take the words that the other person handed you and repeat them back in your own words.

Paraphrasing is a process of *interpreting* another person's statements rather than simply parroting them back. More important, it demonstrates to the other person that you have processed these statements internally. When you are paraphrasing someone, your responses often begin with statements like the following:

- It sounds like . . .
- I can see that . . .
- So you want . . .
- You clearly feel . . .

As we have discussed earlier, statements like these do not imply that you agree or disagree with the other person; they simply mean that you heard and understood them and that it is safe to talk about what they are saying. At the same time, it sends a powerful signal of warmth, acceptance, and understanding to the other person that opens the door to productive dialogue, whether you ultimately plan to accept or challenge their message.

When you are receiving feedback, the power of paraphrasing is best explained in terms of how *you* feel in the split seconds after *you* give someone feedback. If you are like most people, questions like these are probably swirling through your mind in the split seconds after you open up:

- Is he going to pay attention to me?
- Will he get upset or defensive?
- Does he understand what I am telling him?
- Does he care about this issue?

Paraphrasing puts each of these concerns to rest, in a way that creates an open, accepting space for dialogue. More important, it works equally well for any kind of feedback, whether it is positive, negative, agreeable, or disagreeable. Here are some examples of good paraphrasing when people address you:

Feedback	Paraphrased Response
I am not happy about how you treat people on my staff.	It sounds like I've gotten some people on your team upset. Tell me more.
I need you to do a faster job of getting these reports to me.	So you need a quicker turnaround than you have been getting lately.
Did you know that your shirt tail is often sticking out from your pants?	It sounds like I haven't been very careful about how I dress.
How dare you do this to me!	I can tell that you're pretty upset about how you were treated.

Now, listen carefully: In each of these statements, you haven't apologized, you haven't taken blame for anything, and you haven't agreed to change anything—yet. If any of these reactions are appropriate, their turn will come shortly. More to the point, you also haven't lashed back at the person giving you feedback. You have simply lowered the other person's defenses by understanding and welcoming what they have to say. This, alone, will give you both you and the other person more strength and dignity in any feedback discussion, no matter what its outcome.

Step 2: Listen

After you paraphrase what the other person has to say, the next step is something that is extraordinarily easy to remember, and extraordinarily hard to do: Say nothing at all.

Once we successfully get into dialogue with another person, we all share a common universal urge to blurt out things designed to defend ourselves. If we are honest with ourselves, most of us recognize this urge as one of our most basic instincts. It feels logical and natural. Unfortunately, it also works completely against us, for the following reasons:

- It shifts the focus from their agenda to yours.
- It doesn't address their original concern.
- It puts the other person on the defensive.
- It instantly vaporizes any good will you have built up with the other person.
- All too often, it serves as a roadblock to effective dialogue.

Compare these two approaches, and you will see what we mean:

Not so good:
Him: I don't like your taste in clothes.
You: Clearly you think I should dress better. But look, there is a reason I choose to dress this way . . .

Better:
Her: I don't like your taste in clothes.
You: Clearly you think I should dress better. (silence)
Her: Yes, we bankers usually wear dark suits to work and you often show up wearing pastel sport shirts and khakis.

Allow me to translate the first response for you: "I don't care what you think and I'm not even going to ask you to explain it." You have just insulted the other person without uttering a single negative word. Moreover, you have created an environment where it may be awkward and embarrassing for this person to give you more detail about what they are thinking. The second response, by comparison, is an open invitation to talk that leads to a valuable exchange of information.

Another key point here is that good listening is a very active, physical process. You listen with your whole body, and good listening is not just a matter of sitting blankly in silence while the other person speaks. By nodding your head, making appropriate levels of eye contact, leaning toward the other person, and using reflecting statements such as "I see," or "Tell me more about that," you create a very mutual and beneficial exchange without saying a word. When you do a good job of active listening, you not only make the other person feel better, but you facilitate more honesty, better information, and most important, a much lower level of heat.

Best of all, you now know exactly how to respond when you are being challenged and can replace fear with confidence. The first part of it is easy. You take the words that the other person handed you and paraphrase them. The second part is even easier: Simply sit back and listen to how the other person responds to your acknowledgment and show responsiveness to what this person is saying. By taking the "easy" way, as opposed to what comes naturally, you will suddenly start finding that even the most difficult feedback situations start turning into rational, productive dialogues.

Step 3: Acknowledge

This is the third in a trilogy of steps that are easy but not natural when you are receiving feedback. And this step in particular will feel like sucking on a lemon if you aren't used to doing it. But it is far and away the most powerful thing you can do when someone is trying to tell you something: Acknowledge and validate everything the other person says. This point is so important that, if I were a schoolteacher, I would have everyone write the following statement on the board 50 times:

Acknowledging someone is not the same as agreeing with them.

Compare what a powerful difference doing this makes:

Without acknowledgment:
HER: That's a really stupid way to do that.
YOU: No it isn't. This is how I usually do it.

With acknowledgment:
HIM: That's a really stupid way to do that.
YOU: You have a point. I can see where some people might think it is counterintuitive to do it this way.

In the first case, you are closing off discussion and denying the reality of what the other person feels. In the second case, you are engaging the other person in an honest and authentic dialogue, *even when you disagree with him or her.* Put another way, you are always on safe ground (in fact, the safest ground possible) when you show people that you accept how they are thinking and expressing themselves by acknowledging them.

Let's put an important myth to rest about acknowledging people: It isn't a limp-wristed, subservient process of acquiescence, nor is it a process of falsely accepting blame to try and make conflict go away. Done correctly, it is a bold, confident maneuver that shines the most brightly in your most critical situations. Take a look at these examples and see what we mean:

Situation	How We Usually Respond	How to Acknowledge
You are being criticized: "You monopolized the last meeting."	We defend ourselves: "I was only trying to get an important idea across."	Acknowledge what frustrates *them*: "I can see where it's frustrating when someone takes up the floor."
You are being personally attacked: "This problem is all your fault."	We fight back: "Look, we wouldn't have this problem in the first place if it weren't for what you did."	Acknowledge that you have upset *them*: "I can tell this bothers you. Let's talk."
You are being unfairly accused of something: "You messed up this project."	We angrily correct the other person: "Listen, I did my part perfectly. It was Andrea who messed things up."	Acknowledge how *they* perceived the situation, before discussing the facts: "This project was a disappointment to all of us. I'll be glad to walk you through what happened."
You are in trouble for doing something ill-advised: "You really should have left the parking brake on the company van before it rolled down the hill."	We make excuses for what happened: "I got distracted by a gang of people nearby."	Acknowledge the gravity of the situation and its impact on the other person: "I realize this was a very expensive accident for the company."

There is no question that it does not feel natural to say the things in the third column. There is an important reason for this: Our instincts mistakenly tell us that acknowledging someone else's criticism at all might make them pounce. In reality, the opposite is true. When we frankly acknowledge people they tend to calm down, and as we discussed in Chapter 10, they tend to get angrier when we defend ourselves. That is why this is a learned skill that gets better with practice. Conversely, we believe that if we ignore their words the problem will magically go away, in much the same manner that an ostrich might try hiding from its enemies by sticking its head in the sand.

The reality is exactly the opposite of this. When you defend yourself and don't acknowledge someone, they push even harder for *their* agenda and respect you less than if you had condescended to respond to them. In actuality, you almost always gain power and credibility when you help the other person feel understood and respected. This is ultimately why acknowledgment, even when you are hearing painful things from another person, is one of your most powerful weapons in dialogue.

Step 4: Negotiate

You may have noticed that the first three steps in this process are all about the listener. And that is important because engaging the listener first is usually the best way, and often the *only* way, to have a rational and productive discussion with someone after they share feedback with you. But now, it's finally your turn.

In general, our reactions to feedback aimed at ourselves take one of two forms:

1. You can see their point.
2. You would rather get pecked to death by ducks than agree with them.

The first situation is, of course, conceptually easier to handle. Ideally, we can agree with whatever they are saying and propose a solution. For example:
You: "You're right, I do tend to like listening to loud music at my desk. Would it be OK with you if I used headphones from here?"

The second case is a little trickier, but also one where the mechanics of what you say are more important than ever. When most people disagree with someone, the answer is usually some variant of "no," and the way the other person reacts to this "no" is often one of the key reasons that difficult discussions escalate into arguments.

This is why I want you to always phrase your responses in terms of what you *can* do. It feels funny, because (a) we are so highly programmed to say "no" to people, and (b) when someone wants X, and we cannot do X, it feels really funny to respond by saying "I can do Y" instead. In situations like these, every fiber of our being wants to talk about what we *can't* do, but by using "can" language, we adopt the posture of an ally and an advocate. Here are some examples:

Situation	"Can't Do" Framing	"Can Do" Framing
Someone wants you to turn their projects around more quickly. You are swamped.	I am way too busy.	I can let you know exactly where you stand relative to my workload.
Someone feels you are too soft with people. You do not agree with her and feel she is like a drill sergeant.	I wouldn't want to treat people like you do!	I would like to hear what has and hasn't worked for you.
Someone wants you to stop challenging him all the time. You feel he does a poor job.	If you don't want me to speak up, you need to work harder.	I agree that you should be treated with respect.

Words and language are critically important in situations like these. They do not absolve you from the need to negotiate in good faith with another person. They also do not guarantee, in and of themselves, that another person will agree with your position. What they *will* do, however, is draw much of the heat out of these discussions. If you aren't used to phrasing your responses in "can" language, you will be surprised how hard it is for people to stay angry with you and how quickly you are both having a rational dialogue—and hopefully, reaching a consensus that benefits both parties.

Taken together, these four skills turn the awkwardness of responding to another person's comments—particularly negative ones—into a thoughtfully composed performance that anyone can learn and practice. They cost you nothing in terms of agreeing or disagreeing with people, and yet they can almost magically lead to greater consensus and stronger relationships. Once these skills start coming naturally, you will discover that procedural skills like these can make other people's feedback painless as well as your own.

PUTTING THE PLAN INTO ACTION

In closing, let's explore how these skills come together in a hypothetical example, designed to show you the rhythm of an effective dialogue when someone is giving you feedback. Suppose that someone is not a big fan of this book. (I am making this example up, of course!) Here is what they might say, and how I would respond using the PLAN approach.

> **Reader:** Hey, are you Rich Gallagher? I just wanted to say that your book stinks!

Step 1: Paraphrase
> **Me:** It sounds like you didn't get what you wanted out of this book. Tell me about it.

Step 2: Listen
> **Reader:** You go on and on about this nonsense about creating painless dialogues and don't just come out and tell people to cut the comedy and change their behavior.

Step 3: Acknowledge
> **Me:** You have a good point. I could see where people get frustrated about not just telling people what to do. And I respect the fact that you took the time to read my book and share your reactions with me.

Step 4: Negotiate
> **Me:** What kinds of things would you want to see in an ideal book?
> **Reader:** I'd like to see you just tell people to shut up and get back to work, like I have to do every day.
> **Me:** Fair enough. Let's take a look at how you normally handle these situations and how you feel it works for you.

As you read this, keep mind that I violently disagree with everything he is saying. But by creating a space where he feels heard and understood, using a procedural approach, we are having a constructive and respectful dialogue that is leading both of us to a productive conclusion.

More important, this process goes far beyond influencing his reactions. I am learning from what he has to say, which is ultimately the whole point of receiving feedback. Even if I don't agree with his basic stance toward using harsh, deficit-based criticism, I learn about what makes people like him tick, and what kinds of responses work best for him. For example, at one of my training seminars, I once spoke with a former corrections officer who politely disagreed with me about always speaking to another person's interest. In his experience, working with incarcerated gang members, he felt it was important for people in his profession to establish authority over people first and then build respect on both sides later. It was a fascinating dialogue where we both learned a great deal, and I might have missed the value of it entirely if I simply defended myself.

Once we learn to roll with feedback from other people, and use a strength-based approach to responding to it, everything starts to change in your relationships with other people. For example, one of my first summer jobs in college was as a stock clerk in a department store. One day at work, a young woman I had never met before turned to me and said out of the blue, "You know, you always shuffle your feet when you walk. You should pick up your feet." I politely acknowledged her, listened to what she had to say, and thanked her for being kind enough to say so. This exchange had several very important benefits for me:

- I stopped shuffling my feet in the stockroom.
- I created a better impression on coworkers who were too polite to say anything.
- She learned that I was a nice person to deal with and that it was safe to talk with or even challenge me.

Beyond these immediate benefits, there was a much more important long-term benefit for my relationship with this coworker: We have now been married for over 30 years! And even when a painless approach to receiving feedback doesn't lead to wedded bliss, it has a powerful impact on all of your workplace relationships. It creates a comfort zone for other people, turns negative feedback into productive dialogue, and helps you stand head and shoulders above most people as a leader. Moreover, it fosters a learning environment where people will use their observations as gifts that make you a better person. In a very real sense, it can turn criticism into pure gold.

Section IV

Putting It into Practice

CHAPTER 13

Case Studies: Creating Painless Discussions in Real Life

T his chapter brings painless communications skills to life for the kinds of difficult but common situations that most of us encounter in the workplace. It looks at several case studies, each of which deconstruct a tough problem using the skills taught in this book. In the process, I am going to open up my playbook from how I and other people handle some of the most common situations with which people struggle and show you how the CANDID approach can almost magically turn each of them into productive discussions.

Here more than ever, I would like you to read this chapter with a pencil and paper in hand. Think about how situations like these translate to the people and situations that frustrate you at work, and start writing down what you would say differently, based on what you are reading here. If you take this simple step, you will finish this chapter with a smile on your face, a renewed sense of leadership, and a newfound strength in how to handle anything that comes your way in the workplace. Now let's dig in.

CASE STUDY #1: DOOBIE-DOOBIE-DOO

Bob is a long-tenured employee in Marketing who performs high-quality work and has an exemplary record of attendance and punctuality. But he has one problem: He is obsessed with the late singer Frank Sinatra. Posters of Frank cover the walls of Bob's office, which is embarrassing to other marketing employees who bring prospective clients on-site, and a CD of the song "Strangers in the Night" plays incessantly while he works. He even recently showed up for work wearing a Fedora hat and a 1960s tie. You are Bob's manager, and his coworkers have demanded that you "do something" about him.

People wear a wide variety of "plumage" to define themselves as individuals. Whether it is music, sports, cultural identity, or even tattoos and earrings, humans beings often like to send out a clear sense of who they are. And most of the time, these kinds of differences are perfectly OK.

Where you run in to trouble is when someone doesn't quite "fit" with their surrounding workplace culture. For example, purple hair dye may look fine at a video arcade, but perhaps not so well among a group of investment bankers. Likewise, a person in a buttoned-down suit might be out of place working at the video arcade. When there is a gap between your "plumage" and everyone else's, the differences can be awkward for everyone, particularly because they tread on personal space, not just job performance.

This situation also touches on what happens when someone is overinvested in something to the point where other people are uncomfortable. When someone at work talks incessantly about his favorite artist, sports team, or political viewpoint at every available opportunity, he may be totally oblivious to how it annoys people around him—and moreover, this person may feel it is his right to express himself as he sees fit. This is why situations like these often escalate to people's managers.

At the same time, I feel this is actually one of the more painless discussions to have with someone, for two reasons: (1) There are lots of safe places to start the dialogue, and (2) there are plenty of opportunities to build mutual respect. These in turn hold the keys to solving this issue painlessly, with good feelings on both sides. Here are the keys to a productive dialogue with someone like Bob.

- Take a learning attitude toward how Bob feels about Frank Sinatra. Perhaps he is simply an overly invested fan, or perhaps Sinatra's music had a fundamental life-changing influence on him in some way. The more you ask, and the more you learn, the more likely you are to find points of influence and negotiation.
- Liberally acknowledge and validate everything Bob has to tell you. Your best chance for change will come if he feels that you understand who he is in the present moment.
- Avoid, at all costs, the "yeah, but" discussion, In other words, avoid any and all variations of "I respect your taste in music, but you are an-

noying other people." Your mindset should be to respect Bob *and* find more productive ways for him to be himself.

Ultimately, you need to break this conversation down further into three distinct phases: Acknowledging and validating Bob's view of the world, normalizing that it is OK for him to feel (but not act) that way, and then negotiating ways to "be himself" that respect other people's boundaries. Let's try this using the CANDID process:

Compartmentalize. Discussing Bob's affection for Frank Sinatra in a nonthreatening way is clearly a safe place to start the discussion because he is doing everything but advertising his preferences on a billboard. So the logical place to start the discussion might be a neutral observation like, "It looks like Frank Sinatra's music means a lot to you." In all likelihood, assuming a modicum of good relations between the two of you, you will have no problem getting a response to this observation.

Ask questions. After Bob responds to your opening, the questions that follow should ideally drill down deeper into what his motivations are, and what he thinks of music in the workplace in general. Depending on what direction he takes the discussion, some questions you might ask include:

- Has Sinatra's style had an influence on your life?
- When did you start listening to his music?
- What do you think about other people's music?

At this point, you are gathering information, not ammunition: Your goal here is to understand Bob better and build a relationship based on mutual respect and empathy. In the process, you will gain valuable insight about how he sees himself and the rest of his workplace, which will in turn inform your responses from here.

Normalize. Bob's like of Frank Sinatra clearly involves more than musical preferences; they are part of his life and his identity. Given that, the most important part of the dialogue is to create a zone of safety for talking about behavior that is driving you up the wall. By doing this and resisting criticism at this point, you open the door to a productive problem-solving dialogue.

In particular, it is critically important at this phase to avoid dry catch phrases like "I understand" or "I see," which risk conveying disengagement or disinterest. Instead take Bob's statements, gift wrap them with your own empathetic paraphrasing, and hand them back to him. Here are some examples:

"You are right. Sinatra certainly did speak to a very important era in time."
"Lots of people identify with an entertainer who speaks to who they are."
"I can see how you feel because I happen to be a big fan of Elton John myself."

Discuss the issue. This part of the dialogue is a little tricky. In general, of course, your goal is to present the facts of the issue at hand, factually and neutrally. But as we mentioned earlier, you should also try to avoid having a "yeah, but" discussion that appears to be a cynical attempt to give lip service to his tastes while still telling him to basically knock it off.

In this case, a little reframing is probably in order. Instead of discussing this as *his* problem that *he* needs to change, consider framing this as a limitation for other people that you are inviting him to help solve. Compare these two examples and see what we mean:

Not so good:
"I respect your tastes in music, but it's not fair to make everyone else listen to a dead crooner all day. And it is a little embarrassing to bring clients here who may or may not like your music. Could you stop doing this?"

Better:
"I respect that the Sinatra style is part of who you are and what makes you unique. Here is the situation I am dealing with: Some people are more sensitive to other people's music than others. And since this is a marketing department, I am concerned about client reactions as well. How do you think we could best keep everyone happy?"

By recruiting Bob as an ally at this stage, while taking the time to understand and respect his life and preferences, you are much more likely to engage him in mutual problem solving, rather than a defensive exchange.

Incentivize. Last we checked, there was no law against being a fan of Frank Sinatra. So what is in it for Bob to tone things down in your workplace?

Most people facing this situation would focus immediately—and mistakenly—about how not annoying his coworkers would "benefit" him. But this is a glorified way of telling him that he is doing something bad and putting him on the defensive. As with any situation, you want to head straight for the tippy-top of the ladder of benefits and start there. Depending on your relationship with Bob, some of the benefits for him changing might include:

- Learning to connect with a broader range of clients and coworkers.
- Gaining respect and authority within his team.
- Discovering how a few reasonable accommodations such as headphones and dressing currently can let him enjoy everything he wants without worrying about conflicts with others.

This brings up an important related issue. What if you go through this process and Bob's response is, "Gosh, I don't think this is much of a problem, and I kind of like the way I am. I would just as soon leave things as is"? Do not give in to human nature quite yet and pressure him to comply. Instead, keep gently engaging him in solving your problems with the other employees. For example, you might say, "I respect that. My greater concern is that this is going to leave a number of people unhappy, and I don't want to do that. How can we resolve this so that everyone is satisfied?"

Do you ever have to ultimately force a solution in situations like this? Sometimes. But be aware that the way most of us approach situations like these, by putting Bob on the defensive, often leads naturally to such an outcome. By changing the mechanics of what you say, and learning to listen to and understand Bob first, you will find that it rarely if ever comes to this point. Follow the process and you will almost always be pleasantly surprised by the outcome.

Disengage. Now jump back in to your normal relationship with Bob and close the discussion by talking about things you have in common, like his work.

Congratulations! You have just navigated a touchy personnel issue while preserving the respect, dignity, and good work of an otherwise talented employee. By ending on a positive note, you confirm a relationship based on mutual respect, and underscore your faith in Bob to ultimately do the right thing. More important, by using a gentle, patient approach, you have painlessly made the workplace a better place for both Bob and everyone else.

CASE STUDY #2: A SMALL MATTER OF PERSONAL HYGIENE

Sally is the receptionist for your customer service center. She is a likable person who tries hard, but she does have one problem: She stinks. Literally. She wears old clothes and showers "whenever," and people notice. As Sally's manager, this bothers you because her job requires her to interact with nearly everyone on the team. Now your team members are asking you to talk to her about the problem.

This situation is often thrown to me as a challenge by people in my workshops: How can you have a painless, strength-based discussion with someone who doesn't "get" basic standards of hygiene?

I have actually been in this situation many times with employees, and it is in fact tailor-made for the approach in this book. The reason it is so challenging for most people is that the subject matter is so inherently personal. Unlike a performance issue that you can dispassionately troubleshoot, or a situation where people's authentic emotions boil over, this is a case where many people feel stuck because they do not see a way to avoid embarrassing and humiliating the other person.

First, let's get one thing clear: This *is* an awkward subject to bring up with other people. But can you talk about it without upsetting the other person? Yes, absolutely. And more important, in my own experience the right approach to discussing this generally leads to both mutual respect and behavioral change.

There are two keys to handling this situation well. The first is that breaking this discussion down in to its component parts is more important than ever, particularly in creating a safe place to start the dialogue. The second is that this situation calls for lots of normalizing because your goal is not to make the other person feel stupid. Rather, your goal is to help her understand that she and other people simply have different norms to be accommodated.

So here is how the CANDID approach breaks down in one of your more candid situations:

Compartmentalize. Where is a safe place to start when someone doesn't shower and smells bad? To answer that, think about whether there are ever any legitimate situations where people get sweaty. I can think of a few: when people are active, healthy, and exercising, or when the weather is hot, or when someone is rushing around a great deal. So that is where I will start the discussion, in a safe place that makes Sally seem normal:

"I notice that people often get active and sweaty when they exercise."

or

"The weather has been really hot lately, and people often get sweaty."

Ask questions. Your next job is to gauge the other person's self-awareness of the problem. So instead of telling Sally that she smells, ask her if she is aware of other people's reactions in a way that is nonthreatening:

"Some people are more sensitive to other people's body odors than others. Have you sensed that this has been an issue from your end?"

The entire rhythm of this discussion hinges around the other person's response to this question. If they are aware that there is a problem, you have created a neutral opening to explore why they let it happen. This could range from a conscious decision to be frugal and save water, to rarely buying new clothes, all the way to a physical problem such as a kidney disorder.

Conversely, if they have no idea there is a problem, you are now easing them in to the idea that other people perceive them differently. This leads to the next and perhaps most important step: normalizing.

Normalize. Once Sally answers you, your response has a tremendous impact on how she feels and reacts, so your job at this point is to pour on the empathy. Here are some examples of how to normalize the things you might hear at this point:

Sally's Answer	Normalizing Statements
I didn't even realize there was a problem.	That is very common. Most of us don't realize how we may smell to others when we are active.
I am pretty militant about saving energy in our household, and so I only shower twice a week.	Lots of people are looking for ways to live simply and save money nowadays.
Wow, do I offend lots of other people?	Don't feel bad. Different people have different thresholds of what they notice in other people.
I've been talking to my doctor for years about this problem and haven't been able to get anywhere about it.	Some people have physical issues that affect how they smell, and I certainly respect that.

Remember, you are not fixing the problem at this point, you are just using acknowledgment and validation to make it safe to talk about it. At this point, two important things should hopefully be in play: You are now in frank dialogue about this issue, and there should be a mutual respect and lack of defensiveness on both sides. Now let's move on to the heart of the discussion.

Discuss the issue. At this stage, your job is to discuss the situation neutrally and factually, and to ask rather than tell, Sally what to do. The exact path this takes will depend on her level of self-awareness, as evidenced by her answers to your question above. Let's look at some examples of where you might take this:

• "Some people are more sensitive than others to how people smell when they are sweaty, and I wouldn't feel bad about it. I just want everyone to be comfortable around you. How do you think we might address this?"

- "This is a very common situation. For example, I often chew gum because I have a dry mouth, and without it I am not always aware if my breath might offend people. Are there things you might do to deal with getting too sweaty at work?"
- "I respect your frugality. If you can balance that with other people's levels of sensitivity, my sense is that everyone would be a lot more comfortable. Do you see a middle ground here?"

These problem statements, each reflecting different responses from Sally, all get the issue on the table very frankly. But they also each do something even more important: They continue to normalize the situation as one where reasonable people simply have different perceptions, which is probably exactly the way Sally saw the situation before you both spoke. Above all, you are also recruiting her to solve the problem in a way that is collegial and nonthreatening.

Incentivize. It is very tempting at this point for most people to cast this situation as a "negative incentive" by making well-intentioned but threatening statements like, "I don't want you to offend the other people on your team." You would get your point across with statements like this, but it would probably also come across as threatening to Sally, which in turn could lead to hostility, defensiveness, or a lack of motivation.

So what benefits Sally here? First and foremost, probably the relationship with her coworkers. Second, she may be thinking about how this situation affects how she is perceived from a career standpoint. So your job here is to speak to these benefits, in the context of this being an easily fixable issue. For example:

"Everyone really likes you here, Sally. As long as you are sensitive to other people's comfort in situations like this, this seems like a very solvable problem."

If appropriate, I might seize the opportunity to stroke Sally's good points such as her work or relationships with coworkers, to help solidify this issue as a minor blip on the radar screen that can be dealt with. Either way, I would be framing this situation in terms of a good overall career from someone who has lots of competencies to create an incentive for her not to offend other people.

Disengage. Finally this situation, more than most, calls for a re-affirmation of a good working relationship. We are in luck in the sense that Sally is already doing a good job otherwise, and switching back to the practicalities of her normal job is a great way to bring a very sensitive issue to a productive close.

I want to make it clear as we wrap up this case study that I have often used this exact approach with people in my own management career, and each time it has yielded precisely the results I wanted: better hygiene *and* a continued good relationship with an employee I respect. Turning sensitive conversations into good outcomes in a way that is ultimately no big deal on either side of the transaction is, to me, the essence of painless communication.

CASE STUDY #3: DOUBLE TROUBLE

Beverly and Steve are both productive employees who do not like each other at all. Beverly is still angry with Steve about the time he reported her to a supervisor for smoking in the office last year, while Steve feels that Beverly is a loudmouth who gets on his nerves. Recently, your customer service department angered an important client by not getting back to him about a problem she reported. It appears that this situation happened because Beverly never responded to a request for information from Steve, and Steve chose not to pursue it any further. You need to meet with them both to discuss the situation.

So what happens in a situation where two people in your workplace are locked in mortal combat with each other?

This situation parallels the classic scenario of family therapy. A family comes in to a therapist for help, and as you go around the room and talk to each of them, they are all equally convinced that the other people are at fault. The mother will claim that the son is a hoodlum, the son will claim that the mother is always getting on his case, the father will claim that everyone ignores him, and so on down the line. Of course, the goal of therapy is not to serve as a glorified referee; it is to help people understand each other and learn new ways to get more of what each of them wants.

This is the same stance you will take with two or more warring employees. When I have faced these situations in my own career, I have found the most effective approach is to work with each employee individually, then have a facilitated meeting between all parties to discuss moving forward. First, here is how you can use the CANDID approach in your individual meetings with each party:

Compartmentalize. This situation is tailor made for what I call the *perfect neutral opening*: You will ask Beverly what bothers her about her relationship with Steve, and ask Steve what bothers him about his relationship with Beverly. I guarantee you will get an earful in both cases! Listen carefully to capture valuable and often subtle cues about how each person interacts with the other one.

Ask questions. Use Beverly and Steve's responses to gather more information about the specifics of their conflict. Be sure to ask each of them how they respond to the other person's provocations.

Normalize. At this stage of the discussion, your goal is to make it clear that you understand and acknowledge each person's frustrations, both to create a safe space for dialogue and to give you the credibility to negotiate a solution.

Discuss. At this stage, the facts of the situation are how their behaviors impact their ability to do their jobs well, as well as how they impact workplace morale. If they respond predictably about what the other person should do, gently keep shifting the focus to how the person you are talking to can handle these situations better in the future, and engage them to come up with their own best solutions for this.

Incentives. Your incentives for each person will revolve around the context of the situation. Aside from the broader issue of workplace harmony, learning to get along better with a difficult coworker can benefit the reputation, productivity, stress level, and leadership of each of these parties.

Disengage. In a situation like this, where emotions run high and there is no shortage of blame, it is important to close the discussion by reaffirming the strengths of that person's value to the team.

Hopefully you will reach a point where the heat has been lowered on both sides, each party feels heard and understood by you, and each person has thoughtfully considered more productive ways to handle the other person in the future—including, hopefully, a little coaching from your end about using more painless communications techniques with each other. Now you are ready to get both people together, in a positive and criticism-free meeting that covers the following ground:

- Validating the value of both people to the team and the importance of their working relationship
- Acknowledging the past frustrations between the two of them, while sharing that you understand and respect these differences
- Asking both parties how they plan to move forward from her, and validating their responses
- Expressing confidence in their ability to work things out from here and congratulating them both for being willing to talk frankly and resolve these issues

In my experience, situations like these do not tend to involve a clear "good" person and a clear "bad" person; rather, they tend to erupt from an accumulation of personality and work style differences, which in turn leads to a dysfunctional relationship. As a third party, you have the ability to both mediate their issues and model the kinds of communications skills that they can both use themselves. By using a painless approach with both parties, individually and jointly, you can help these people both change the way they look at their working relationship, and positively impact their own conflict resolution skills for the future.

CASE STUDY #4: THE CUSTOMER IS ALWAYS RIGHT

Les is a longtime customer of your printing press. He is demanding, but pays well, and has given your company a small but steady stream of business over the last few years. Today he is calling you wanting a rush job. Because he feels he is such a loyal customer, he wants you to waive the 50 percent rush premium you normally charge for these jobs. You have discussed this request with your boss, and she says, "No way."

We haven't discussed many customer issues so far in this book, for an important reason: Our focus is on difficult conversations with people you work with, where you have a vested interest in their attitudes and behavior. Customer situations tend to be short-term transactions with people you have little influence over rather than a long-term relationship.

Customer situations have their own dynamics, many of which I explore at length in my previous book *Great Customer Connections* (AMACOM, 2006), but this situation more closely resembles an ongoing workplace relationship because of the length of time you and Les have been working together. Moreover, it is not without risk: If you do not communicate well, you run a much greater chance of losing his business. So let's look at it through the lens of using the CANDID technique:

> *Compartmentalize.* There are safe and unsafe parts to this discussion. The safe parts include things like what he needs and the nature of his deadlines. The unsafe parts are saying "no" to what he wants and your policies in general. So start the conversation by acknowledging his time urgency and letting him know you want to learn more about the project.

> *Ask questions.* Use Les's responses to ask good follow-up questions about what he needs and when, with a particular eye toward what is most time-critical.

> *Normalize.* Acknowledge and validate everything Les says, ranging from his sense of time urgency to his tenure as a customer.

> *Discuss.* Frame the discussion in terms of how you can best make Les happy, based on what you have learned. Use phrases such as "I wish" and "even though" to move from what you *can't* do to what you *can* do. For example:
> "I wish we could waive the rush premium, especially since you've been working with us for a long time. Even though we have too many jobs in the pipeline to do that, let's see what we can do to help. Would a partial order help you meet your deadline?"

Incentivize. What benefits Les about working with you even if he has to pay more? Here is where you can sell the benefits of your working relationship and then engage him about what he would prefer. For example:

"I don't want to see you have to line up another printer with a deadline looming. If you have the budget for a rush job, even for a partial order, we can help you meet your deadline with the kind of quality you expect from us. What would work best for you?"

Disengage. As with any workplace situation, one of the best ways to end a tense negotiation with a customer is to shift back into the small talk that normally typifies your customer relationship with Les.

Customer transactions and difficult workplace situations do share one thing in common and that is the need to speak to another person's interests from their frame of reference. In this case, you are trying to turn an inappropriate demand from ruining what has been a productive customer relationship, by using the same approach you would use with a demanding employee: Acknowledge what he wants and negotiate what he needs. This serves as an example of how painless communication skills can filter into situations outside the workplace, and even provide some benefit to your personal life.

A WORD ABOUT BULLIES IN THE WORKPLACE

I would like to close this chapter by shifting from fictionalized case studies to a situation that is all too real for many people in the workplace: how to deal with bullies in the workplace.

When we were young, bullies were people who threatened us physically. Today they may be executives in tailored suits, or foremen on the shop floor. According to a recent poll by the Workplace Bullying Institute and Zogby International in late 2007, over a third of employees report being bullied, half of them to the extent that it affects their health.[1] That represents a lot of misery out there.

At the same time, there is a real dearth of information on how to understand and manage these situations when they are actually happening to you. Type "dealing with bullies" in your favorite Internet search engine and, to no one's great surprise, you will get nearly a quarter of a million hits as of the last time I checked. But here is the real surprise: type in the exact phrase "what to say to a bully" and you will get very few hits and very little useable advice as of this writing.

Why is there so much silence on such an important subject? Because bullies are often seen as one-dimensional enemies to simply be fought or avoided. As a result, nearly all of the advice currently out there revolves around the legalities of handling bullies: documenting specific abuses, when to speak with your human resources department, what your legal rights are, and the like.

Perhaps a more balanced view comes from the government of South Australia, which has strict legal protections against workplace bullying. A recent report from them describes workplace bullies (the majority of whom are supervisors) as people who often lack basic management skills and do not know how to behave differently, are compensating for a sense of personal inadequacy, or perhaps work in a negative culture where bullying is seen as a normal management style.[2] In these cases, the solution is often seen as an educational as well as a legal issue.

Of course, some bullies cross the line into inappropriate behavior, like one supervisor described by a blogger as someone who knocks over filing cabinets to make a point. (I have a good three-word technique for this situation: Call the police.) Others may be sexist, racist, or out to exploit power for their personal gain. But for others—perhaps the majority—I honestly feel that the right communications skills can help defuse these situations and build mutual respect.

Here is my view: We tend to view bullies as evil villains, and this view colors our responses. But bullies generally respond to being challenged the way most of us do. They fight back and rationalize that you are the problem. If you change the script of what you say, you can often change the outcome, particularly if you speak to their interests while maintaining your own dignity and boundaries. So here is my advice on how you can adapt the CANDID approach to situations with the garden-variety, non-sociopathic office bully:

1. Start the conversation in a safe place by acknowledging and validating the bully's underlying agenda, *not* his or her behavior. For example:

- When someone has an angry outburst, say, "I can tell by your tone of voice that you are pretty upset."
- When someone has been spreading rumors about you, say, "I understand you have some concerns about my performance" or ""I understand you aren't happy about what I said to Sally."

- When someone is pressuring you to do an unrealistic amount of work, say, "It sounds like we are under a lot of deadline pressure. Tell me about it."

Yes, it feels funny to talk like this with someone who acts like a jerk. It goes against all of our gut instincts. And no, it doesn't always work, particularly when things cross the line into discrimination or abuse. But perhaps 70 percent of the time, this will get you into productive dialogue. Try it and see what happens.

2. *Ask nonthreatening, factual questions about the situation.* The natural tendency of people to push back when they are challenged is magnified even more in people who seek to get their way through intimidation. So when you ask situational questions, you are both yielding the floor and holding them accountable at the same time. For example:

- "What would you have liked me to do instead?"
- "How would you have preferred that I handled things with Sally?"
- "Tell me more about what our clients are expecting by the deadline. Do we have any flexibility with them? Could I speak with them directly and see how we can help?"

With responses like these, you are not simply "knuckling under" to the bully's anger; you are showing interest in the bully's issue while at the same time making him responsible for the facts that he claims are behind his behavior. Statements like these serve as the roots for how you start turning intimidation into dialogue.

3. *Set boundaries while offering to address the bully's agenda.* Bullies usually fight back when they are challenged, but a surprising number of people will respect you for standing your ground if—and this is a big if—you also speak to their interests. For example:

- "I don't want to see you upset and I don't want to be yelled at in the future. Where can we go from here?"
- "I don't want you to feel criticized, and I also want to be free to be honest with other people. How can we solve this in the future?"

- "I want to make the client happy, and I feel I can honestly do X much work between now and then. How should I best use my time between now and the deadline?"

I feel that everyone is entitled to a workplace that is free from harassment, and I fully support legal protections designed to put an end to workplace bullying. But in the meantime, I also feel that in many cases your communications skills can make a big difference in stopping these situations in their tracks. Here is a good, quick litmus test: Does anyone in your workplace successfully stand up to the bully, or get picked on less? If the answer is yes—and this in no way excuses the bully's behavior—you may find that communicating differently can help you gain more power and respect in a situation that makes most of us very uncomfortable.

With each of these case studies, my hope is to not only show you examples of how to resolve these specific issues, but to get across a larger and much more important point: Painless, strength-based communications skills can help you deal with even your most difficult workplace situations. Moreover, you do not need to be blessed with great wisdom or skills to manage these situations. Just take out a pencil and paper, write "C-A-N-D-I-D" down the side of the sheet, and let the process go to work for you.

I see this process in much the same way that most of us view driving a car. A century ago, automobiles were rare and exotic machines, and someone who could drive was held in high esteem, much like a jet pilot is today. Nowadays, we tend to hold people who can defuse difficult workplace situations in a similar esteem, as special people who are different from the rest of us. In my view, we now have the tools to allow *everyone* to handle difficult situations painlessly, in the same way that many of us now have driver's licenses. So keep practicing these skills, and happy driving!

NOTES

1. Workplace Bullying Institute, "U.S. Workplace Bullying Survey," September 2007, http://www.bullyinginstitute.org/zogby2007/wbi-zogby2007.html.

2. Interagency Roundtable on Workplace Bullying (Australia), "Factors and Impact of Workplace Bullying," July 25, 2008, http://www.stopbullyingsa.com.au/factors.asp.

Troubleshooting the Mechanics

The process outlined in this book is remarkably effective in most situations where you need to engage someone in dialogue. But what about when someone clams up and won't talk, or tries to stab you in the back, or has little or no motivation to negotiate with you?

Most of us try to address situations like these *emotionally*, but the reality is that even tough roadblocks in communicating with other people can be dealt with *procedurally*. This chapter discusses some of the most common situations where people often need to "modify the script" of standard strength-based feedback in ways that still help produce effective dialogue in even the most difficult cases, cases such as:

- When someone won't talk to you
- When you are feeling sabotaged
- When there is too much anger
- When you have no leverage with the other person
- When there is a crisis

Let's take a look at each of these situations and see how you "modify the script" of your basic feedback skills to manage even some of the toughest situations in communicating with other people.

TOUGH SITUATION #1: SOMEONE WON'T TALK TO YOU

At first glance, it would seem that communications skills are very hard to put into practice when the other person is not communicating. But a person who does not speak or respond to you is, in fact, communicating very strongly. Here are some of the things this person could be saying by his or her silence:

- I feel threatened by you and do not want to say anything right now.
- I am going to frustrate you by holding power over whether we talk or not.
- I need to think things through and cannot reply immediately until I think my response over.
- I have social anxiety and am uncomfortable being confronted.
- I am offended by what you said and do not want to acknowledge it.

Silence can be a very frustrating response, particularly in a sensitive conversation that you were not looking forward to having. But in most cases, you will still have a better outcome by responding with a strength-based approach. Let's look at what most people say in situations like these, break down how others process these statements, and see why this is the case.

"Let's talk about this later." There is nothing wrong with this statement on paper, except that other people universally process this as a provocative and confrontational statement. When you say this, what they are actually hearing are things like:

- "You have a problem because you are not talking to me."
- "I will decide when we eventually address this."
- "I am going to force you to speak to me sooner or later."

Think carefully about the times you have used this statement in the past. I suspect you will discover that you have rarely if ever received a positive response to it. Even though you probably will, in fact, address the situation later, talking about this up front pushes your response from safe to unsafe territory.

"Are you uncomfortable talking about this right now?" This is another statement that may seem well intentioned but is in reality another mine-

field. If the other person *is* uncomfortable, you have just shined a 300-watt spotlight on his or her discomfort and done exactly the opposite of what they are hoping you will do, which is respect them and go away quietly. Even worse, they may not be uncomfortable at all; they may, in fact, feel angry or confrontational. In this case, you have just denied the reality of how they feel, and made them—you guessed it—more upset with you.

"What's the matter?" When people will not respond to you, particularly in a sensitive situation, one of our first impulses is to gather information about why this is the case. As we have discussed earlier, asking appropriate questions is often a good thing, but only when these questions are based on the other person's interests, and ideally, on what the other person is telling us. When you start asking questions to someone who is uncommunicative, however, you have just crashed a party to which you have not been invited. Far too often, the result is more silence or pushback.

So what *do* you say in a situation like this? In my mind, there is only one effective, strength-based response to the silent treatment: Acknowledge their right to be silent. Here are some things that might be safe to say in this case.

- "You don't have to talk right now if you don't want to."
- "I respect your feelings. If you'd like to talk later, I'm here."
- "I will follow your lead about when you want to talk about this."

Then resist all temptation to try to arrange a later meeting, discuss the issue, or talk further about the other person's silence. You have gently lobbed the ball back in their court, given them power over the dialogue, and made it safe for them to talk when *they* feel better about it. In the process, you have given yourself more power and respect, not less.

As for restarting the discussion, you now have the knowledge that this is a sensitive issue for the other person. You can now use this knowledge to let time pass, and to approach the next discussion gently—perhaps by electronic mail, which gives the other person time and space to respond, or with a more safe opening the next time you approach this person face-to-face.

Speaking of power, let's discuss an interesting and important wrinkle to this situation. What if this person giving you the silent treatment happens to be your subordinate?

In a situation like this, you have the right to force a discussion, at least in principle. Refusing to talk with one's superior is technically insubordination. But think carefully about whether you should use this power. If you are dealing with a critical situation that cannot wait, do whatever you have to do with class and dignity. But in most cases, giving someone time, space, and even a little power is a much more effective approach even when you are the boss. Remember that your goal is to create buy-in, not resentful compliance.

Once, for example, I tried to talk with an employee about repeated failures to respond to customers—a critical requirement of her job—and when I asked her to explain what had happened with the latest customer, she responded by slamming the door of my office and storming off. I could have technically followed after her and insisted on continuing the discussion, but I doubt it would have been productive at that point. Instead, I waited until the very end of the day when we had more privacy, and I led off the discussion by asking how things were going for her. Even though she was formally warned to do her job in the future—or at least talk to me about it—we still had a productive and respectful discussion, and she never had a performance problem afterward.

Remember also that situations like these often need to be reframed before you jump to conclusions about them. Once, for example, an employee was transferred on short notice into my department, and when I met with him for the first time, he responded in monosyllables and never even turned around to face me.

For many people, this kind of response would be taken as being highly disrespectful, particularly from a subordinate. But in that moment, I chose to roll with it and not make an issue of it. For one thing, while I knew nothing about this person, I knew many people who suffered from social anxiety and found it very uncomfortable to interact with people. For another, when I spoke with other supervisors later, I learned that this was a very common pattern of response for this person. So I never made an issue of it, politely spoke to the back of his head during our first meeting, and made a mental note to approach him gently and respectfully in the future. He ended up being an extremely successful employee and we had a great working relationship.

Silence is often much more powerful than any words we can use. You should be very careful about using it in your own interactions with people because of the strong reactions it can stir up in others. But when you are confronted with it from other people, move past your own reactions to it and use the moment to give the other person more power in the dialogue. In most cases, the rewards will come back to you many times over.

TOUGH SITUATION #2: YOU ARE FEELING SABOTAGED

Before we examine this issue, let's define "sabotage," which is a very emotionally charged term. Is the other person doing things like slashing your tires or stealing money from your purse? If she is, this is not a situation for strength-based communication. This is a situation for what I call the "three-word technique:" Call the police, talk to human resources, consult your lawyer, and the like.

But I am guessing that this person is not, in fact, slashing your tires. Instead, she is probably gossiping about you, trying to show you up, or making herself look better than you to the boss. These are all situations that are A-OK for handling with a painless, strength-based approach, and in point of fact, it probably represents the only way to change the other person's mind and behavior.

Think about the last time you were a brat, perhaps when you were very young. You got caught at it and your parents or teachers punished you. What kinds of thoughts were running through your mind? Contrition? Remorse? An epiphany of good behavior for the future? If you were like most people, anger and revenge was probably more like it.

It is here, in this space, that the roots of many acts of sabotage are born. A coworker feels you act better than she does, or that you do not approve of her, or have put her in her place, so she takes action based on her own personal law of the jungle. This is important to realize because you know from your own experience that fighting back directly against this kind of mindset accomplishes nothing other than hardening the other person's resolve, or worse, pushing her deviousness further underground to more subtle levels.

Other forms of sabotage may not be reactions to you personally, but rather to what you represent. You may be successful, likable, and well respected by people, and this threatens people who see you as blocking their path, or who feel that they never get the same kind of respect that you do. Here as well, the dynamic is the same: The harder you push, the more the other person hardens his or her position.

Am I going to propose some limpid, Pollyanna response to someone who is attacking you behind your back? No. But I am going to ask you to put your anger and frustration in the back seat for the moment, do a little bit of reframing, and then walk with me through a strength-based approach that can change this dynamic for good.

First, let's get out a sheet of paper, write down what the other person is doing or saying, and try to unpack the real message behind her behavior. (And I'll give you a hint, it is more about the other person than it is about you.) Here are some examples:

What They Are Doing	What You Are Thinking	What the Other Person Is Thinking
Boasting about her work and tearing yours down to others.	He is attacking me!	I am worried that people don't respect my work as much as yours.
Tattling to the boss about your mistakes.	She is attacking me!	I need to be in the boss's good graces, or else I might become a target.
Withholding critical information.	He is attacking me!	I don't want you showing me up.
Gossiping and criticizing you behind your back.	She is attacking me!	I am trying to ingratiate myself to others and look better in their eyes.

Here is a hint: If you talk about the issue in column two—namely, how the other person is attacking you—you are done for. You stand no chance whatsoever of changing the other person's mind. Once you shift over to column three, you start opening up some possibilities for a new relationship, which is ultimately the only effective way to stop the backstabbing.

Let's take what we have learned from this process and roll it into the CANDID technique for structuring a dialogue with the saboteur. Here are some of the things you can say in this process:

Compartmentalize: Create a neutral opening around issues like, "Are there issues that frustrate you about us working together?" or "Are you worried about what the boss will think about your project?"

Ask questions: Take the other person's answers—*not* your own feelings—and turn them into questions that show interest and concern. For example: "What do you want people in management to know about your work?"

Normalize: Acknowledge and validate everything the other person is saying. For example, if the other person is honest enough to share her frustrations with you, respond with statements like, "I can see that it gets annoying for you when the boss seeks me out first."

Discuss: Here you get to hit the issue right between the eyes. But remember, facts, not emotion. For example, "It bothers me when you get frustrated and say things to other people about me. I don't want you to be unhappy about our working relationship. Where can we go from here?"

Incentivize: This part is simple. If there is something in it for her, you have a chance to change the dynamic between the two of you. If there isn't, you don't. Come prepared to help *her* succeed in some tangible way, and say so: "I would like to see you get more credit for your work in the future, and work as a team with you. You have a lot of talent, and I'd like to see it get appreciated." And what if she is a poor employee as well as a backstabber? Find incentives to help change that. "I'd like to help you find a niche where you can be successful."

Disengage: You have probably been biting your lip so hard through this process that there are teeth marks in it. After all, you are trying to understand and help someone who has been targeting you. You have some very real frustrations about what has happened between the two of you. And now is not the time to discuss them. Talk about work, the team (no more gossip, please), or her friend's baby shower, and shift back into the rhythm of the normal work day.

Speaking to the interests and incentives of a backstabber goes against everyone's human nature. But with a little luck, and a lot of planning, you have a much better chance of creating a new working relationship than any of the 98.5 percent of people who would simply confront her. And however things turn out, you will have taken the high road and gotten your message across.

TOUGH SITUATION #3: YOU FEEL TOO ANGRY

First of all, congratulations for being honest with yourself. None of us are made of steel. There are situations that are so important to me that it would be hard to address them rationally—such as someone threatening a loved one—and there are situations like this for you as well. Congratulations for being willing to explore how you might respond in cases like these. Understanding yourself and your boundaries is not only OK, but very important.

Second, take a moment to examine your objectives. Do you want to make the situation better, or do you simply want to punish the other person?

Sometimes you do, in fact, just want to punish the other person. When someone steals your car, it is time to call the police. When someone has been embezzling from your company, the proper place for that discussion is probably a courtroom. And when your spouse or your family is at risk, you must protect them. When important boundaries are being crossed, you are beyond the realm of communications skills.

But let's suppose that you aren't dealing with behavior that would merit a stretch in the state penitentiary. And let's also suppose that you do, in fact, want to improve the situation if it is at all possible. This is the place where you can start changing the script of what you say.

Ironically, while high-emotion situations are among the most uncomfortable to deal with, they are also among the easiest to manage using strength-based feedback, as long as you remember the following golden rule:

Your feelings should always become your facts.

Once we get to step four of the CANDID process—where we discuss a situation neutrally and factually—there is no limit on being totally frank with people, *as long as you suck the emotion out of it first.* In other words, talk about how you feel about a situation without *acting* on how you feel about the situation. Here are some examples:

Situation	Typical Reaction	CANDID Reaction
Someone did not follow through on an important commitment.	I can't trust you!	There were consequences for me when you did not meet this commitment.
You were promised a promotion, but your management changed their minds at the last minute.	How dare you go back on your word like that!	I want to understand why the promotion you promised me did not happen.
Someone yells at your receptionist.	No one talks to my receptionist that way!	I was concerned about the language you used with my receptionist.
Your boss just asked you to cancel your family vacation.	You are being totally unfair to me!	This vacation is very important to me. Let's talk about what is happening at work.

Do you notice a couple of things in common with each of these responses? The more angry "typical" reactions involve or imply the word "you" and end with exclamation points, while the more factual reactions all start with the word "I" and do not. When we are upset, most of us lead with the other person's faults, but I want you to get better results for yourself by sticking to the facts of the matter.

When you get to the point of the discussion that you are laying the issue on the table, these emotional "facts" will take you much further in dialogue than anger, criticism, or threats—even though every inch of you is probably feeling far from accommodating.

One other important point here is knowing when you need to scrap the step-by-step process that we outline in this book. Painless dialogues are thoughtfully composed performances that require advance planning and a mindset of speaking to another person's interest. Being honest with yourself about the times that you simply cannot do this helps you boil down the conversation to its basics: namely, expressing your concerns in a way that is as neutral and factual as the circumstances allow.

Above all, practicing using painless dialogues in your normal daily business life will serve you well when the stakes are higher for you. Learn the gentle art of replacing raw emotion with productive logic in your everyday conversations and you will find that the right words will be there for you when you need them.

TOUGH SITUATION #4: YOU HAVE NO LEVERAGE

I have good news and bad news for you. First, let's get the bad news out of the way. There are few if any communications skills that can make people do what they do not want to do. When a telemarketer calls me (usually at dinnertime) about a hot new investment opportunity, and I hang up on them, it is not the fault of their script. I simply do not want what they are selling. Even if Zig Ziglar or Winston Churchill were on the other end of the line, I would still be hanging up on them. (Oh, alright: If I knew it was Zig Ziglar, I would probably stay on the line to learn from his sales techniques. Then I would hang up on him.)

Now, here is the good news: Getting your colleague to change has little or nothing to do with how much authority you have over him.

Let me ask you a frank question. How many people do you know who have made real, substantive changes in the way they behave at work? I will wager this is a very small number of people. Now, here comes the more important question: *Why* did they change?

If you look critically at the number of people who have truly changed, I suspect that most of them saw some tangible benefit for changing. Perhaps someone paid attention to them, mentored them, or saw potential in them. Or they learned a new skill that gave them renewed faith in themselves. Or they discovered an opportunity that was important to them. Am I right that most people who changed fall into this category?

How about the people who were simply being pressured to change by people like superiors or others who have authority over them because they were deficient in some way. Did they all change? Here I will wager that most of them either stayed the same or got fired. Again, am I correct?

If you are like most people, this short and unscientific survey should hopefully give you a sense that authority is not usually what makes other people change problem behavior. In fact, authority usually only ensures compliance for behaviors that are *not* a problem, such as when you or I are asked by our bosses to do a routine task. By comparison, here are some of the things that *do* cause other people to make positive changes:

- There is something in it for them.
- They like you personally.
- They feel it will serve the greater good.

In other words, the tools of motivating another person to change are often sitting right in your hands. By corollary, most failures in getting someone to change boil down to one of two reasons. The first reason is the same reason that I hang up on telemarketers: the other person sees no benefit in changing. But the second reason is why most people fail: they only speak to their own interests and get rejected.

So let's say that your office mate, Herman, is a grumpy sort who takes forever to complete tasks that hold up your own work. He does not report to you, probably never will report to you, and does not exactly lay awake at night worrying about your deadlines. Going to him and pressuring him to speed things up will probably get you nowhere. Now, let's take a look at how you might use each of the three principles above to get what you want.

Having something in it for him. Can you benefit Herman in some way? Are there things you are good at that you do to make his life easier? If the answer is yes, you have a possible bargaining chip to get what you want. If you focus your CANDID discussions around trying to understand his agenda, and then link your help to getting what you need, you may have what Humphrey Bogart once called "the beginning of a beautiful friendship."[1] For example, if you finish paperwork much more quickly than Herman can, you might offer to rearrange your responsibilities to help him, as long as he meets your deadlines. If you are averse to doing more work to get what you want, perhaps you can give priority to something he needs.

Get him to like you personally. Do you feel that building a good relationship is impossible with someone who makes your life difficult? Let me tell you about one of my experiences with someone like that.

Dealing with the Dragon Lady

"We call her the Dragon Lady," I was told as I started a consulting project many years ago. "She doesn't get along with people and takes her sweet time getting anyone's projects done. Don't say we didn't warn you."

When I went over to introduce myself, I first noticed and admired a picture of a sharp-looking young man on her desk, and she responded with obvious pride about her son and his career. Then I brought up the project I needed from her. Here is what I said:

- I told her that I respected what a tough job she had, and how people must be very demanding with someone in a role like hers.
- I acknowledged and validated her comments about how much pressure she gets put under from other people.
- I asked what would be convenient for her, as I explained what I needed.
- I thanked her sincerely and told her that I was looking forward to working with her.

When I came back that afternoon with a completed project in hand, my consulting manager was amazed. "How did you manage to do that? We never get anything from her the same day! You must have been really lucky."

I wasn't lucky at all. I treated someone with respect who wasn't used to getting any from most of the people she worked with—just ceaseless demands. More important, for the remainder of our time together, I thought that she was an absolutely great person to work with. By the time the consulting project ended, I couldn't help but wonder what things would be like for the rest of the company—all nice people in my book—if they took a little extra time to get to know her as a person.

Meanwhile, you don't need an organized campaign to get someone like Herman to like you and perhaps ultimately help you. Just look for small opportunities to compliment the things he does well, recognize his agenda, or speak to his interests. Relationships evolve in those small moments of truth that we experience every day with each other, and small kindnesses given without an agenda can often come back to you in unexpected ways.

Find the greater good. This one is a little trickier because companies have tried to get their employees to support their interests since long before a mission statement was ever invented. While appeals to company productivity often fall on deaf ears, getting people to believe in something greater than themselves can create incredible results.

In 2006, new manager Jim Leyland began spring training by telling his Detroit Tigers—a last-place baseball team for the previous three seasons—that he wanted them to "walk around with the swagger of World Series champions."[2] The results were a team that dominated all of baseball for most of the year and ultimately did play in the World Series. And in my own management career, where I have seen customer contact operations that I have led achieve near-perfect customer satisfaction ratings and near-zero turnover, changes often started with a simple challenge to become the very best team in our industry—and a game plan to back it up.

So how does this all relate to you and Herman? If you have a dream that could benefit the both of you, perhaps his productivity might become a small price to pay to help achieve it. Perhaps you and he might teach the company a lesson about how your jobs are done. Maybe there is a goal that would bring newfound visibility to the both of you, or perhaps there are recognitions you can both strive for, such as conference presentations on your work.

Whatever you suggest must of course benefit both of you, and more important, Herman needs to buy in to these benefits. But if you can tap in to a mutual opportunity that engages both parties, getting what you want may fall in as part of the package deal.

The common denominator in each of these three cases is that there are simple, practical ways that almost no one ever practices that can change the dynamics of many workplace conflicts between peers. The most effective way for people like Herman to give you what you want, leverage or no, is to create the kind of relationship where Herman *wants* to help you. If you learn the mechanics of speaking to another person's interests, and deliver them in a way that is authentic and honest, you will look at the concept of influence and leverage in a whole new light.

TOUGH SITUATION #5: COMMUNICATING IN A CRISIS

By this point, you hopefully have a good sense of how to create a painless dialogue for common workplace situations. If someone is annoying, late, snippy, or domineering, you now have the tools to be all over it. But what if you had a high-stakes, life-death crisis to deal with? For example, what if someone was threatening to commit suicide?

I have, in fact, been trained to talk to suicidal people. Years ago I served as a telephone crisis-line counselor, and it was a wonderful life experience that I would recommend to anyone. And perhaps the most fascinating thing about it was learning that a very structured process of communication that could be taught and practiced by anyone was remarkably effective when I was on the phone with someone who was experiencing a crisis. By following these steps, it was almost magical to watch these situations turn around to become a rational discussion focused on taking productive next steps.

The reality is that our most critical life situations, like hostage negotiations, crisis interventions, and post-trauma counseling, involve procedural techniques that share many things in common with the approaches in this book. Concepts such as starting conversations in a safe place, acknowledging and validating how people feel, reframing, and taking the emotion out of difficult statements are now all part of the evidence base behind our most critical conversations. The next time you hear about a police SWAT team negotiating with a barricaded suspect, be aware that there are more similarities between this situation and what you say to a coworker who constantly spills her coffee than you might think.

I am not going to attempt to teach you the details of crisis communication in this chapter because these skills deserve more than a passing mention in a few paragraphs. My own training as a crisis counselor involved several weeks of classes, role-playing sessions, and guest lectures from experts ranging from police officers to psychotherapists, and every minute of it was valuable. If I could boil down the most important concepts into useable advice, the key points include creating a safe space for people to share whatever they are feeling without judgment or "advice," providing lots of acknowledgment and validation, explicitly checking for how safe the other person is, and focusing on concrete steps in the here and now.

At the same time, I do want to close this section on troubleshooting difficult situations by sharing that even the most difficult crisis situation can be understood and managed using trainable skills. If you find this area as fascinating as I do, I would like to recommend that you drink more deeply from the courses and volunteer opportunities that are out there. You will not only learn to help others, but benefit your own life in ways that you never imagined.

YOUR GUT: YOUR MOST IMPORTANT TOOL
FOR DIFFICULT CONVERSATIONS

We have spent a lot of time in this chapter and this book talking about what to do with your mouth. But ultimately, one of the biggest tools in managing difficult feedback situations lies in using another part of your body: your gut. Once you become comfortable with the mechanics of how to have painless dialogues with people, your gut is a very effective tool in determining when to move forward, when to hold back, and when it is perhaps best to retreat and live to fight another day. Here are some examples where your gut will serve you much better than your communications skills:

- If someone has been having performance problems at work and his wife just gave birth to a child, or has just learned she is battling health problems, it is probably best to trust your gut and table the discussion for another time, no matter how longstanding these performance problems have been.

- When your own manager has just expressed a lot of frustration about you or your work, your gut may be telling you that this is not the time to approach her about a raise or a change in working conditions.

- When someone seriously crosses the boundaries of other people or of society, you may be dealing with a situation in the "15 percent" category we mentioned earlier in the book. If someone has embezzled money, assaulted someone, or committed a serious case of sexual harassment, your gut may be telling you it would be better for your human resources department or the police to be using *their* feedback skills in this case.

- In one case that made the national media a few years ago, a man brought his daughter in for Take Your Kids to Work Day where both he and his child were greeted with the news that he was being laid off. Some people at this company probably should have trusted their gut here, if not their calendar.

Or there may be situations where the other person hasn't done anything, said anything, experienced a major life event, or robbed a bank. But you just have a funny feeling that you aren't going to connect with this person or that the situation could turn into a confrontation. Listen to that funny feeling. Then go back to your desk, pull out a slip of paper, write C-A-N-D-I-D down the side of it, and workshop what you would say. Work hard to think about what would benefit the other person and come up with the best neutral opening you possibly can.

If that funny feeling starts to be replaced by confidence, then communications skills can probably help you here. If not, try to analyze what the dynamic might be between the two of you, perhaps with the help of some outside feedback. You may need other skills here, like political astuteness, a trusted intermediary, or a gently worded e-mail. Trust your gut first and then draw on your skills.

That said, I want you to understand that the vast majority of even the most difficult situations—in my view, at least 85 percent of them—can be dramatically changed by the words you use. Start from a mindset of what the other person wants and needs and then trust yourself to acknowledge, validate, and seek reasonable solutions that benefit both of you. Even the most challenging discussions involve a process that you can learn and practice, and when you master that process you will gain a newfound confidence that will stick with you for the rest of your life.

NOTES

1. Michael Curtiz (director), *Casablanca* (movie), Warner Brothers, 1942.

2. Associated Press, "Tigers one game from World Series," October 14, 2006.

Epilogue: Summing It All Up

What are the limits of good communications skills?

I would be the first to acknowledge that choosing the right words will not solve every problem in life. They will not make other people suddenly become smarter or more competent. They will not change another person's personality, nor will they impact their likes or dislikes. And they may not always change someone's entrenched personal beliefs.

I also agree that there are situations whose gravity will overwhelm even the best communications skills. In the workplace, particularly with the level of change going on today, decisions are made that can have severe impacts on people's lives. As a former crisis counselor, I know that the right words can be extraordinarily powerful in even our most difficult times, but do not mistake that for the false belief that you can talk your way out of anything.

Yet most of us barely scratch the surface of what we could accomplish in our most difficult situations. We are all just a few short words away from generating more goodwill, more cooperation from others, and much more of what we want. And all we need to do to tap in to this vast reservoir of success is make some simple changes to what comes out when we open our mouths.

You may listen to some people and think they are nice, or empathetic, or diplomatic. You may think they exude leadership and a sense of being in control. You may feel that they simply work better with other people. And you wish that somehow, you had whatever "it" is that makes them so comfortable in their own success with others.

I see these people differently, because I am constantly deconstructing the mechanics of what they say. To me, their success can be expressed in very procedural terms. What you see as a different attitude, I see as a thoughtfully composed performance. More importantly, I see their success as something that can and should be yours.

When I sit down with workplace groups and teach them the secrets of painless communication, it is truly amazing to watch these talented people change the way they sound and act. At the beginning of the class, people assume that I am somehow nicer or more skilled at handling tough situations. But then as they start using the same techniques themselves, you can feel the heat draining out of the room, and soon the vast majority of them suddenly start sounding as nice—and as productive—as I do. Same people, same personalities, different words—and very different outcomes.

While the field of strength-based psychology is fairly recent, its principles have been working for people since the dawn of time. At a personal level, this lesson was driven home for me very powerfully when I was a young engineering supervisor at a major aerospace company back in the 1980s. In those days, I saw the world very simply. Success revolved around your technical competence, and the more technically skilled you were, the better. Then I joined this firm, which had literally thousands of engineers, and noticed something fascinating. The people who got ahead, many of whom were relatively young, were the ones who could communicate their ideas well to others.

This was a powerful and life-changing lesson for me. As I rose through the management ranks of my own technical career, becoming a software executive with a director-level position by the time I was 30, it was clear to me that a conscious decision to learn to communicate well had more to do with my success than bits and bytes. But more importantly, it would be many years later until I learned how a positive strength-based approach to coaching and interacting with other people would have a dramatic impact on *their* performance.

Since then I have watched some truly amazing things happen as myself and others have made the conscious decision to "go painless" in our daily communications with others. I personally helped turn around the performance of a 24-hour call center to create near-perfect customer satisfaction ratings and near-zero turnover as its manager. Among the thousands of people I have trained in the years since then, I have seen entire departments transform their reputations from surly to superstars, and individuals develop a newfound joy and confidence in what they do. And nearly everyone I have had the pleasure of working with comes away seeing their relationships with others in an entirely new light.

So why doesn't everyone take part in this wonderful world already? In my mind, there are three basic reasons:

1. *It takes practice.* Nearly every time I lead a class, I have a student who describes him- or herself as a "people person" who loves interacting with others. But when I have them role-play a difficult situation, they often say exactly the same non-painless things most of us do when we are under pressure. Are they hypocrites? Not at all. Painless communication comes naturally to a very lucky few of us, but for most of us, we have to be taught and coached the mechanics, just like when we learn to drive or play sports. The pull of human nature is very strong, and it takes purposeful effort to overcome it.

2. *Our culture hasn't caught up yet.* Turn on your television, read a blog, or pick up a newspaper, and you will see a lot of less-than-painless communication out there. Look at goals and mission statements in the workplace and you will often see them cast in competitive or even military terms. And even on the home front, far too many people belittle each other in ways that will keep the psychotherapy profession alive and well for a long time. We sadly live in a society that thrives on confrontational discourse, and if there is a silver lining to it, it is that learning to communicate painlessly can give you a strong competitive advantage over what many of us hear and model.

3. *Words aren't everything.* Type the word "boss" and "jerk" in your favorite search engine, and see how many hits show up; last I checked it was over 3 million. So if communications skills are so important, why do so many people who communicate poorly still end up in leadership positions? The answer is that leadership is often defined by functional skills rather than interpersonal ones, and not all leaders are necessarily the best at what they do.

At a deeper and perhaps darker level, many people are put into positions of authority because of their ability to drive performance by making people uncomfortable. Does high-pressure leadership create results? In the short term, you bet it does. But if my own experience is any guide, if you look critically at the turnover, poor motivation, and infighting of a high-stress work environment, my sense is that this style of communication is like driving with one foot on the accelerator and one foot on the brake.

At the same time, there is now a growing realization of the strategic importance of communicating painlessly with people. For example, the Joint Commission that accredits hospitals in the United States has recently started requiring its hospitals to have a code of conduct and communications skills training for their staff. This is due in part to a growing amount of evidence linking hostile communications and medical errors.[1] Similarly, a *Harvard Business Review* piece entitled "More Trouble than They're Worth" examined the economic and business impact of people who are confrontational with the people they manage, a concept that later led to a bestselling book.[2] Increasingly, we are measuring the value of how we speak to others in financial and not just emotional terms.

I truly believe that we are at the dawn of a new era of how we communicate with each other, one that will change the way we live, work, and solve problems together. It will create better workplaces, better relationships, and perhaps even world peace. These skills fit within the larger context of a strength-based movement that is now sweeping psychotherapy, athletic coaching, and business performance, a movement that keeps growing as we discover the incredible benefits it offers us.

These benefits are yours for the cost of a piece of paper, a pencil, and a sincere desire to learn and practice a new way of listening and speaking. In the process, you will discover that truly painless communications—the kind that speak to the interests and feelings of other people while respecting your own limits and boundaries—represent the most effective way to get what you want in any conversation, with any person, in any situation. My hope is that they will also serve as the next steps in your personal path toward success and fulfillment, and it has been my pleasure to join you on this journey.

NOTES

1. JoNel Aleccia, "Hospital bullies take a toll on patient safety," MSNBC.com, July 9, 2008, http://www.msnbc.msn.com/id/25594124/.

2. Robert Sutton, "Breakthrough Ideas for 2004: More Trouble than They're Worth," *Harvard Business Review* (2004), 83(2): 19–20.

The Painless Conversation Worksheet

T his section presents a simple worksheet for planning the specifics of a difficult workplace conversation, using the CANDID technique described in this book:

- *Compartmentalize* the message to create a neutral opening.
- *Ask questions* based on the other person's response.
- *Normalize* the situation.
- *Discuss* the details—factually and neutrally.
- *Incentivize* the outcome.
- *Disengage* from the discussion.

Step 1: Compartmentalize the Message to Create a Neutral Opening

First, break the message into its safe parts and unsafe parts. Safe parts are those areas where the other person will not disagree with you or get defensive (e.g., how this person feels about something, or the mechanics of doing his or her work).

What are the safe parts of this message?

_____

_____

_____

Next, use this "safe" content to choose a neutral opening based on one of the following four forms:

- *Have the other person describe what happened*, particularly when something has gone wrong.
- *Ask the other person how he or she is doing*, particularly when you notice a change in behavior.
- *Make a neutral observation*, particularly you notice negative dynamics between people.
- *Use the "I" technique*, where you relate things to your own behavior or observations, particularly when someone has made a mistake.

What will you use as a neutral opening?

_____

_____

_____

Step 2: Ask Questions Based on the Other Person's Response

After the other person responds, ask questions to gather information about the other person's viewpoint and feelings, in a neutral, blame-free atmosphere. Good questions should be *relevant, empathetic*, encourage *open answers*, and *paraphrase* the other person.

How do you expect the other person to respond to your neutral opening?

_____

_____

_____

What kinds of questions can you ask the other person to engage him or her, based on his or her responses?

_____

_____

_____

Step 3: Normalize the Situation

Make it safe for the other person to talk about the subject by *normalizing* each of their responses, using one of the following three forms:

- *Acknowledgment:* You recognize the other person's feelings.
- *Validation:* You accept the other person's feelings as being valid.
- *Identification:* You identify yourself or others as having experienced the other person's feelings.

What kinds of responses do you expect the other person to have?

_____

_____

_____

What statements can you use to normalize these responses?

_____

_____

_____

Step 4: Discuss the Details—Factually and Neutrally

Discuss the issue, frankly and completely, using a three-step approach:

1. Take the *emotion* out of the issue with a factual, neutral description.
2. *Engage* the other person in solving the issue.
3. *Empathize* with each and every response.

Even with very sensitive or difficult issues, keep the discussion on a factual level, use engagement questions to keep the other person in dialogue, and use empathy to acknowledge—not necessarily agree with—the other person.

What is the most factual, neutral description of the situation?

_____

_____

_____

What can you say to engage the other person, once you have discussed the situation?

_____

_____

_____

How will you empathize with the other person's responses?

_____

_____

_____

Step 5: Incentivize the Outcome

Frame the outcome of the discussion in terms of the *strongest possible benefit* to the other person, using areas such as the other person's likes and dislikes, hopes and aspirations, and values. Avoid "negative benefits," such as avoiding punishment, if at all possible.

What do you feel would be the greatest benefit(s) to the other person for changing?

_____

_____

_____

Step 6: Disengage from the Discussion

Shift the discussion away from the issue, and back into the rhythm of your normal working relationship. Focus on areas such as normal work issues, common interests, or the future.

What can you say to disengage effectively from the discussion?

_____

_____

_____

Strength-Based Psychology:
The Basis of Painless Communication

Years ago, the field of psychology—and for that matter, human relations in general—revolved around the deficit-based model that we discussed earlier, the focus of which was on fixing what was wrong with oneself. You received psychological treatment if you had problems, you were sent to anger management classes if you were angry, and you went to marriage counseling when you and your spouse were at war with each other. In recent years, a new *strength-based* movement has been gaining popularity, first changing the way we do psychotherapy, later changing the way we deal with people in fields ranging from business and sports, and much more recently, influencing the way we communicate with each other.

Strength-based psychology, also known as positive psychology, has little to do with the similarly named self-help movement of positive thinking. (For one thing, the former has a distinguished Ivy League–based research center to its name, while the latter is more commonly associated with motivational speakers and pop psychology.) It represents a very pragmatic and well-researched focus on how people use their strengths to grow and change. For example, while therapists of a generation ago might look for hidden conflicts, today's strength-based therapists focus more on what skills and competencies people have right now, and how to build on them.

Today, the strength-based approach has become one of the fastest-growing models for psychotherapy, particularly in disadvantaged populations that often grow up hearing negative messages about themselves, which has a negative impact on their self-worth. More recently, the strength-based psychology movement

The Roots of Strength-Based Communication:
Changing the Way We Do Counseling

Picture this: You have a teenage single mother who lives in a poor neighborhood. She has recently split up with an abusive boyfriend, she has no job, and her children are in foster care because of his abuse. If you were a social worker treating this woman, what kinds of things would you say to her?

Some people might look at this as a case of someone with problems who needs to be "fixed." But listen to what the late Insoo Kim Berg, one of the key figures of the solution-focused brief therapy movement, had to say to this woman in a clinical demonstration:

> "(You) got out of that relationship? Wow! I wonder how you did that?"
> "Where did you learn to be such a good, loving mother?"
> "Let's say . . . a miracle happens (and) the problem that you brought here is solved. How will you be able to tell that?"

In short, Berg quickly narrowed in on this woman's strengths, and used them to engage in a dialogue about how she could build on these strengths to get her children back, and move forward with her life—goals she soon accomplished after this therapy session.*

*Source: I.K. Berg & P. DeJong. "Solution-Building Conversations: Co-Constructing a Sense of Competence with Clients." *Families in Society: The Journal of Contemporary Human Services, 77*(6), 376–391 (1996).

has started to make inroads into the business world, with the advent of books such as the bestselling *Now, Discover Your Strengths* by Marcus Buckingham and the late Donald Clifton.[1] Books like these are based on a bold premise that for the most part, you shouldn't waste time trying to "fix" your weaknesses, but rather that you should understand and play to your strengths. Similarly, many of the key managers of major sports teams—where the financial stakes for excellent performance run higher than ever—now use a coaching approach based on building on strengths and mechanics, rather than yelling at people to "motivate" them.

Today, the strength-based approach is starting to find its way into the science of how we communicate with each other. Amazingly, given that human beings have been talking with each other for 50,000 years or so (and presumably grunted and shook their clubs at each other long before that), it has only been in recent history that we have started to look critically at the mechanics of how we communicate and influence each other. It wasn't that long ago that both published advice and actual practice often revolved around "letting it all hang out," with an underlying premise that direct feedback was tied in with establishing power and control over people. Nowadays, common wisdom about difficult conversations has become kinder and gentler—and more effective—by focusing on acknowledging the other person, and then telling them how we feel about the situation. In the process, we are now learning that mutual respect and acknowledgment of strengths is a very powerful force for effective dialogue.

A SIMPLE BUT LIFE-CHANGING IDEA

Against this backdrop, this book introduces a fairly radical notion: taking the issue of how *you* feel almost totally out of the equation of a difficult conversation. Why? Because both my experiences "turning around" the performance of workplace teams, and the tenets of strength-based psychology, teach us something truly amazing: how you feel is much less important than *what benefits the person to whom you are talking*. In other words, dialogue works best when *every single word* somehow benefits the other person.

In this book, I have given you an approach to difficult conversations that is designed to never—yes, *never*—put people on the defensive or make them feel guilty. In the process, you will tap into powerful forces that will keep the other person in dialogue and move them closer to making positive changes in their attitude and behavior. If like most of us you aren't used to speaking to people this way, it will feel funny and take practice at first. But once you master this skill, both your confidence in any interpersonal situation and the level of influence you have with other people will both change dramatically.

So will this approach leave you in some namby-pamby world where no one can ever do anything wrong and the sun shines every day? Not quite. Anger and punishment do have an appropriate, logical place in any workplace, based on what these emotions were biologically designed for: to protect ourselves when important boundaries are being crossed. So if someone is stealing from your workplace, sexually harassing employees, or threatening to slash someone's tires, go ahead and feel upset; you have my blessings. But in most cases, when you are dealing with everyday job performance issues where mistakes or emotions or lack of motivation get the better of us, a strength-based approach will not only work better, but *dramatically* better. And believe it or not, even in cases where you have to do things like set boundaries or discipline someone, you can still use a strength-based approach to make these situations as humane and productive as possible.

This new way of speaking to people is more than just a process; it is a life-changing way of looking at how we view and interact with people. It almost magically changes your relationships with others, all for the price of a few simple changes to the mechanics of how you communicate. Learn and practice this approach, and you will gain much more than just effective communications skills—you will gain the personal confidence and leadership that comes from truly knowing how to tell anyone anything.

NOTE

1. Marcus Buckingham and Donald Clifton, *Now, Discover Your Strengths* (New York: Free Press, 2001).

Index

About the Author

Rich Gallagher is a former customer service executive who heads a training and development firm, the Point of Contact Group, in upstate New York. He is a leading national authority on communications and customer skills, and has been dubbed "one of the founding fathers of modern customer support" by one of its leading professional societies.

Rich is the author of several previous books on communications skills and workplace culture, including *What to Say to a Porcupine: 20 Humorous Tales that Get to the Heart of Great Customer Service* (AMACOM, 2008); *Great Customer Connections: Simple Psychological Techniques that Guarantee Exceptional Service* (AMACOM, 2006); and *The Soul of an Organization* (Kaplan, 2002). He also served as the subject matter expert for the American Management Association's successful *Communication Boot Camp* training program.

For more information and content on painless workplace communications, visit this book's web site at www.HowToTellAnyoneAnything.com. To learn more about training programs for your own workplace, contact the Point of Contact Group at www.pointofcontactgroup.com.

CPSIA information can be obtained at www.ICGtesting.com
Printed in the USA
LVOW07s2145260515

440025LV00004B/275/P